Style and Authenticity
in Postmodern Poetry

For John —

new old — old new
friends with
utmost affection,
gratitude and
admiration,

29 September 1991
Lake Charles, La.

Style and Authenticity in Postmodern Poetry

Jonathan Holden

University of Missouri Press

Columbia, 1986

Copyright © 1986 by
The Curators of the University of Missouri
University of Missouri Press, Columbia, Missouri 65211
Printed and bound in the United States of America

Library of Congress Cataloging-in-Publication Data

Holden, Jonathan.
    Style and authenticity in postmodern poetry.

    Includes index.
        1. American poetry—20th century—History and
criticism. 2. Poetics. I. Title.
PS325.H58   1986   811'.52'09   85–20966
ISBN 0-8262-0600-X (alk. paper)

∞™ This paper meets the minimum requirements of
the American National Standard for Permanence of Paper
for Printed Library Materials, Z39.48, 1984.

For permissions, see p. 189.

Acknowledgments

Most of these essays have been published previously. For permission to reprint them, I wish to thank *New England Review/Breadloaf Quarterly*, for "Postmodern Poetic Form: A Theory," "The Abstract Image," and "Poems versus Jokes"; *Seneca Review*, for "The Contemporary Conversation Poem"; *Field*, for "Pinsky's *The Situation of Poetry* and Imagistic Convention"; *Ohio Review*, for "Poetry and Commitment"; *Poetry Review*, for "The Paradox of Achieved Poetic Form"; *Georgia Review*, for "Poetry and Mathematics"; *Denver Quarterly*, for "Landscape Poems"; and *American Poetry Review*, for "Style, Authenticity, and Poetic Truth." Thanks also for the support of the National Endowment for the Arts. Special thanks to my friends, who have seen me through the writing of these essays and have offered indispensable suggestions and encouragement: Tom Dillingham, Steve Heller, Reg Saner, Syd Lea, Scott Cairns, Fred Pfeil, F. D. Reeve, Arthur White, Phyllis Morrison, and (most specially) my brother, Stephen—to whom this book is dedicated.

J. H.
Manhattan, Kansas
February 1986

Contents

Acknowledgments, *v*

Introduction, *1*

I. The Uses of Convention

    1. Postmodern Poetic Form: A Theory, *9*

    2. The Contemporary Conversation Poem, *33*

    3. Pinsky's *The Situation of Poetry*
       and Imagistic Convention, *45*

    4. The Abstract Image, *58*

II. The Live Form

    5. Poetry and Commitment, *75*

    6. "Discovered Form" and the Structure
       of Intention, *92*

    7. The Paradox of Achieved Poetic Form, *111*

III. The Use of Poetry

    8. Poetry and Mathematics, *131*

    9. Landscape Poems, *145*

    10. Poems versus Jokes, *161*

    11. Style, Authenticity, and Poetic Truth, *170*

Index, *187*

Permissions, *189*

Introduction

Why, if the intent were not scholarly, might a literate American in the mid-1980s have recourse to the art of poetry? Under what circumstances? What would this person expect of poetry or want of it? What *should* we expect of it or want of it? That is the composite question dwelling behind the eleven essays which make up this book.

To put the question another way: if we single out and examine poems in the contemporary tradition, what do their specific uses seem to be when the conventions which comprise that tradition are well used?

"Convention." That word invokes the grounds from which all of these essays have evolved: my conviction, based on half a lifetime of studying and writing, of teaching and being taught poetry, that, like painting, folk music, tale telling, joke telling, or cinema, like every other art developed to the level of self-conscious sophistication, the "poem" is a blatantly artificial convention; and that like the conventions which define each of the arts—TV soap opera, for example, or country-and-western music—poetry evolves to serve specialized uses that cannot be as efficiently served by other means, uses which, I might add, are not merely academic and exegetical.

The essays comprising the first third of this study propose a rough map of contemporary American poetic convention, speculate on some of the reasons behind these latest forms of evolution, examine in some detail the most prevalent type of contemporary poem—the "conversation poem"—and then, in separate approaches, consider some of the implications in the most recent major event in the contemporary tradition, the decline of imagistic poetic convention in favor of conventions which readmit to favor more abstract styles of discourse.

Descriptions of poetic convention enable us to acknowledge types of poems and to anticipate—even to deduce—

some of the formal problems of composition that might be associated with each type; but such descriptions necessarily ignore issues of literary quality. It is easy enough to approach issues of quality *negatively*. We can judge, perhaps, whether or not a poem has managed to avoid certain obvious pitfalls such as the "fallacy of imitative form." Similarly, generations of students and poets have been trained to explicate, through appropriate tactics of indirection and by employing a sophisticated critical vocabulary, the "statement" which a good poem makes, even while acknowledging that the better the poem is the less satisfactory such a translation can be when weighed against the poem's own language. Such translations inevitably imply reasons for poetic quality, but to positively and thoroughly "explain" these reasons is another thing entirely, bringing us face to face with questions about how to talk about poetry at all.

For any one who has seriously attempted and taught poetic composition, it should be self-evident that the effect upon the reader of a fully achieved poem can be no more rationally explained or methodized than, as a composer and musicologist friend of mine maintains, "any haunting melodic line" could be. In his words, "There is simply no formula for that." It is precisely this issue which, in "The Figure a Poem Makes," Frost rather slyly broaches when he writes, "The figure [of a poem] is the same for love." By "love" Frost means lovemaking; and when, in that same little essay, he maintains, "No surprise for the writer, no surprise for the reader," he is extending this figure, comparing implicitly the relation between poet and reader to the relation between two lovers in the very act of love, an activity whose joyous "surprise," at its highest, most people know better than to try to explain *too* thoroughly. Similarly, most critics know at what point in their analysis of a poem to shut up. Those who do not have long constituted a familiar literary type, a type famous for its misuse—though "abuse" might be a better word—of intellect, and a type which poets and novelists have dealt with rather severely over the years. The character Casaubon in *Middlemarch* is one example of this type, deadening in his fastidiousness. Hawthorne's cold, prurient scientist, Chillingsworth, is another. The speaker of Coleridge's "Dejection: An Ode," though a sympathetic character, is another, so caught up in "abstruser musings" about the creative process that he is in danger of stopping his own creative process; he is in danger of being paralyzed by self-reflection. More recently, in a poem which remarkably foreshadows the limbo of contemporary High-Theoretical discourse, there is the dried-up protagonist of Eliot's "Gerontion."

"The Live Form," then, is about the ticklish business of trying to describe—to find appropriate words for—the power of any good poem, without abusing exegetical discourse. There appear to be some major snags that we run into when practicing exegetical discourse; and to avoid them we must appreciate and be willing to accept some fundamental paradoxes. One is that, if the success of a poem depends as heavily as it seems to upon unforeseen events—upon unpremeditated discoveries arrived at during and, indeed, *by means of* the act of poetic composition itself—then "explication" of a good poem should duly emphasize the revelatory nature of the poem's statement. But is it even possible to explicate the revelatory without transforming it into static doctrine, mere "meaning"? Whether or not it is, these essays try to keep in view constantly my feeling that exegetical discourse is never valid as an end in itself. It should only be invoked as a means to an end—as a way of pointing toward a mystery—much as Wittgenstein at the conclusion of his *Tractatus* suggests logical discourse may, while acknowledging its limits, point toward things about which it is best to remain "silent." Although the events which happen during poetic composition can only be guessed at by the alert reader and can never be observed directly, a good poem embodies an immediate sense of these events. It comprises, in effect, a record of them, delivering to the reader an authentic sense of that record in its original immediacy, even though the accuracy of the record can never be rationally or empirically verified.

A second paradox, one foreshadowed in this book's opening essay, is that the fully achieved poem satisfies requirements which are such perfect contradictions of one another that the poem's success can never be accounted for in terms of rational consistency; it cannot be systematized; it will forever elude theory. But as my explications of specific poems try to persuade the reader, perhaps it is possible, by means of demonstration instead of assertion or argument, to make believable judgments about the quality of those poems. Instead of trying to judge a poem by means of some systematic theoretical approach, it may be more prudent and more appropriate to approach it without too many preconceptions, as an empiricist—to approach the poem curiously and singly the way a botanist wading out into a field and happening upon a peculiar flower might pause to measure, sniff, and draw it, before attempting to theorize.

The act of observing a flower that has been singled out, like the act of studying a specimen of good poetry, is deeply participatory. It requires that the student imaginatively *be* the flower, at least to some extent. Likewise, reading poetry well requires the reader imaginatively to *be* the poem, in the sense that he must create it anew. As the discussions of individual poems in "The Live Form" seek to illustrate, a close reading of a poem may evoke, if only implicitly, a sense of the action— the choices—which went into the poem's original composition; for the sophisticated reader is not a passive one. With each successive reading, this reader will vicariously reenact some of the authorial drama of the poem's original composition, much as a student of mathematics, studying a proof or a word problem, might suddenly "get it," recognizing and completing the same connections which its original inventor had discovered, thereby recapitulating some prior creative process.

The theme of poetic discovery, explored in "The Live Form," leads inevitably, I think, to consideration of poetry as a form of action—moral action—and this is the theme explored in the final four essays, which attempt, by examining specific examples, to narrow down what *type* of action this is—what are its aims?—and thereby to suggest, in terms of function, the outlines of poetry as a genre. "The Use of Poetry" compares the function of poetry to that of other "genres"—to the "genre" of mathematics, to the "genre" of the joke, but also, implicitly, to all other "genres"—asking what kinds of aims are served by a good poem which no other genre, no other specialized language, could serve as well. It suggests by means of examples how the different genres may comprise a sort of "ecology," in which the specialized function and subject matter of each member has evolved with respect to that of every other member.

The issue of the "use" of poetry is, I think, inherently polemical, though perhaps "political" would be a word equally apt. Cultural history is a history of competition, Catholic versus Protestant, for example. The issue is always the same: simply the question of whose daydream shall prevail. The process by which the canon comprising any cultural tradition at any given historical moment has been defined is nothing if not political; and the issue of the "use" of poetry, like the "use" of prayer or liturgy, embodies profound and inherent implications about audience, style, content, format, and authority. Although the essays which comprise this book were arrived at unsystematically, when viewed all together they will be seen to evince certain allegiances on my part, especially my allegiance to what I find myself calling, in lectures and in conversations, "a vernacular poetry of personal ethos," a low mimetic mode of poetry whose tradition leads from Whitman and Wordsworth through Hardy and Frost to such contemporaries as William Stafford, Richard Hugo, and Denise Levertov. This is not the only type of poetry I like. The essay "The Abstract Image" gives an admiring explication of an Ashbery poem, even though Ashbery's "use" of poetry often seems to me too limited—an Olympian, noncommittal language-play that refuses engagement or to make value judgments, poetry that issues from a universe in which one never has to go outdoors or discipline a child or change a tire, from a universe consisting entirely of texts. Yet when I choose to amuse myself in the ludic, whimsical, lyric weathers of discourse, I read Ashbery. Similarly, as the essay "Poetry and Mathematics" indicates, I am attracted to the poetics of Paul Valéry, even though I do not agree with him. As that essay also indicates, even though the poetry of Wallace Stevens would seem to be entirely antithetical to the mode of poetry to which I throw my main allegiance, I love some Stevens poems enough to give them the best form of praise I can give any poem—my most deliberate and curious attention.

But the majority of the poems given such attention in these essays are poems whose "use" is closer to my loyalties, poems in which I recognize my own life and which furnish a subtler vocabulary for my experience than I could have had without them. These poems are not exclusively about their own language or their own formal properties. They are not narrowly personal or confessional; neither are they impersonal. They evoke some sense of an authorial presence behind their words. More than that: this presence, this personality is better than what we are accustomed to in daily life. We sense a substantial, personal ethos behind the language, that the rhetoric is in the service of serious and worthwhile intentions. This authorial presence is one we trust. It is sincere. It may be, by turns, subtle, compassionate, daring. It is not narrowly self-involved. It is not self-pitying or whiningly confessional. It is the presence of a person who can be playful, who has ranged widely in experience and who turns out to know a few things that we had not. These people have faced the usual adversities squarely; and, although they may have been hurt, they were nowise cowed or totally intimidated. They remain unusually interested in the world, alert. They have evident courage, no little wisdom, and now, in poems eloquent enough to be their own sufficient argument, they pass this on to us. If these essays accomplish anything, I hope it will be to introduce readers to good poems which, without a critical context, might have eluded their notice; for that is the sole reason why I study criticism of contemporary poetry: to discover good poems by having them illuminated before me by somebody who got there first, to have my vision, my appreciation, enlarged. The goal of these essays, then, *is* the poems which were their occasions and which remain their raison d'être: that each poem, as it is subjected to the tenderest partial translation that I could manage, might finally win the reader over on its own terms.

I

The Uses of Convention

When you start to write, you carry to the page one of two attitudes, though you may not be aware of it. One is that all music must conform to truth. The other, that all truth must conform to music. If you believe the first, you are making your job very difficult . . . .

—Richard Hugo

1. Postmodern Poetic Form: A Theory

To appreciate the difficulty a critic faces when trying to find any kind of continuity in contemporary American poetry, one need only thumb through the third edition of A. Poulin's anthology, *Contemporary American Poetry*. It would seem at first glance that the poems of John Ashbery and Imamu Amiri Baraka would have nothing significant in common—no more, certainly, than the graceful, late-modernist, domestic verses of Richard Wilbur have with the chants of Allen Ginsberg— both featured in that anthology—or the male boastings of James Dickey have in common with the recent work of Adrienne Rich. Critics have, of course, tried to locate a pattern in this diversity; but their efforts have tended to be incomplete, limited either by methodology or, as in the case of Harold Bloom, by bias. A good example of methodological limitation would be the following ambitious passage by Jerome Mazzaro, from his preface to *Postmodern American Poetry*:

Without the technical language of the structuralists, the formulation of the essential differences between "modernism" and "postmodernism" becomes: in conceiving of language as a fall from unity, modernism seeks to restore the original state often by proposing silence or the destruction of language; postmodernism accepts the division and uses language and self-definition—much as Descartes interpreted thinking—as the basis of identity. Modernism tends, as a consequence, to be more mystical in the traditional senses of that word whereas postmodernism, for all its seeming mysticism, is irrevocably worldly and social. Rather than T. S. Eliot's belief that poetry "is not the expression of personality, but an escape from personality," postmodernists propose the opposite.

Brilliant as this approach is, it is incomplete. Mazzaro's proposal that "postmodernism accepts the division" simply ignores the poetry of Robert Bly, Galway Kinnell, James Wright, Gary Snyder, and other contemporary poets working in the romantic tradition which Paul Breslin has aptly named "psy-chological pastoral." When, for example, at the close of "Late November in a Field," James Wright says,

> I have nothing to ask a blessing for,
> Except these words.
> I wish they were
> Grass.

he is, to use Mazzaro's language, "proposing silence or the destruction of language." In short, Mazzaro's formulation simply does not apply to a significant segment of postmodern American poetry. More troublesome, however, is Mazzaro's assumption that the character of poetry is determined not by evolving convention but primarily by epistemology, by the way in which the poet "conceives of language." Nowhere in the paragraph above does Mazzaro suggest why or in what way the conception of language as a "fall from unity" might be more significant for a *poet* writing in verse than for any other educated user of "language."

Harold Bloom's approach, in *The Princeton Encyclopedia of Poetry and Poetics*, is, like Mazzaro's, epistemological, but it is much narrower because Bloom is trying to define the contemporary tradition according to his taste, to assert a canon which would exclude all but the latest strains of American transcendentalism. According to Bloom, "The *stance*" of "the strongest and most characteristic poetry of the late 1960s and early 1970s, a transcendental synthesis of the various native strains," ignores the "bogus" issue of whether to write in closed or open "phrased fields," and, "in order to escape the fall into the confessional," performs "a deliberate curtailment of the revisionary impulse toward an endlessly journalistic scrutiny" of the self, "while simultaneously [à la Emerson] asking the fact for the form." Bloom then adduces some poetic instances and remarks, "Every passage, whether in tone, in cognitive aim, or in human stance, shows the same anxiety: to ask the fact for the form, while being fearful that the fact no longer has a form." If we translate Bloom into plain English, he means to say that the mainstream of postmodern poetry shuns confessional, strives toward organic form, and is therefore transcendental, part of a tradition that goes back to Emerson. Leaving aside the fact that the confessional mode is very much alive and, in the hands of poets like Carolyn

Forché and Louise Glück, important, Bloom's thesis, while it embraces Ammons, Ashbery, and a few other poets, ignores so much of our best poetry and so radically misrepresents the creative process—a process which is not, as Bloom would portray it, primarily philosophical—that it remains unconvincing.

Postmodern American poetic form, from the political invective of a Baraka to the elegant assemblages of Ashbery, is *not* founded on epistemological anxiety; nor is it primarily "organic." The anxiety which it reflects is anxiety with respect to poetic *convention*: what kind of discourse seems suitable for verse (without sounding obsolete) and what does not? How do you know, particularly when you are writing free verse, when you are writing poetry? Deprived by the modernist revolution of any sure sense of what poetic form should be, poets have increasingly turned to nonliterary analogues such as conversation, confession, dream, and other kinds of discourse as substitutes for the ousted "fixed forms," substitutes which in many cases carry with them assumptions about rhetoric that are distinctly antimodernist. Indeed, it is through deployment of such relatively "personal" analogues as conversation and confession that a substantial number of our poets are attempting to recover some of the favorable conditions for poetry which had seemed to obtain before the triumph of modernism.

*   *   *   *

In order to fully appreciate this analogical impulse behind much contemporary poetic form, one must understand why and in what ways the advent and eventual institutionalization (in universities) of "modernism" has rendered the poetic vocation so much more specialized than it once was. How relatively complacent that vocation had been—how reasonable the assumptions behind it had sounded—is vividly evident in the late Robert Hillyer's aesthetic will and testament, the book-length essay *In Pursuit of Poetry* (1960). Hillyer, born in 1895 in East Orange, New Jersey, was eight years younger than Eliot and ten years younger than Pound. Like Eliot, he attended Harvard. Like most of the founders of American modernist poetry, he spent time in Europe: he was an ambulance driver with the French army from 1917 to 1919. But he remained a traditionalist. It was well after the period which has come to be known as "High Modernist" when the *Collected Verse of Robert Hillyer* (1934) received the Pulitzer Prize for Poetry. And when in 1944 Hillyer retired as Boylston Professor of Rhetoric and Oratory at Harvard, he was considered an important American poet.

A striking aspect of *In Pursuit of Poetry* is the bitterness with which Hillyer attacks modernism. He deplores the modernists' specialization of poetry, evidenced to him by the rise of the New Criticism, and he laments their usurpation of the genteel tradition to which he belongs:

Though the symbolism of T. S. Eliot's poetry and the incoherence of Ezra Pound's *Cantos* have served as damaging models for young men, the more nearly complete sterilization and confusion of recent American poetry were accomplished by the New Criticism.

He attacks the modernists' formal innovations such as "free verse," comparing it to "a river the banks of which are removed so that it spreads out without restraint into a marsh," and he rejects what might be termed the pessimistic vision of most modernist poetry, chiding Eliot for his "*self-pity*, a dreadful element in any art," and Auden for being, in such poems as "'Miss Gee. A Ballad,' completely *heartless*":

This general rejection of humanity, this stripping away of a mystery and aspiration is the result of a materialistic, mechanistic point of view so closely allied to the self-destructive elements of the age that the poet's complaints about them become a colloquy between the pot and the kettle. . . . To mention the human soul in the presence of such poetry would be embarrassing.

The traditionalist conception of poetic form which Hillyer proposes has a cut-and-dried quality that any postmodern poet might envy; for Hillyer's conception of the universe provides the very model for traditional poetic form, for meter:

Intricate though verse seems, it is a more natural form of expression than prose. Verse means a turning, and since the turn must come full circle on itself, we speak of it as a repeating, or recurrent, rhythm, just as in music. Prose rhythm is non-recurrent; hence, verse is more natural because it is closer to the rhythms of the universe—and note that *universe* means a concerted turning . . . we are metrical creatures in a metrical universe.

Hillyer's notion of poetic form and his defense of what we now call the "fixed forms" follow immediately from his view of a "metrical universe":

The main forms . . . have developed through centuries and are the result of endless experiment. Their roots go as deep as the languages, and those that we still have with us are so natural that they might almost be cited as examples of Darwinian survival of the fittest. How foolish it is for defenders of free verse to maintain that these metrical structures are not natural. Free verse has no roots at all, and is itself an unnatural departure from the ebb and flow of all things.

Hillyer classifies the language of poetry into two styles, "the *rhetorical*, heightened and dignified, and the *conversational*, informal and familiar. . . . Each has its dangers as well as its virtues; the first may become bombastic, the second prosaic." The poet's choice of a style must be governed, Hillyer says, by the idiom that is "considered most appropriate for the expression of his idea." Similarly, if—as Hillyer suggests—poetry may be loosely classified into "epic, dramatic and lyric," then certain meters are appropriate to certain modes: blank verse to the English-language epic and dramatic modes, "three- or four-stress verse and divided into stanzas" to "pure lyrics." Hillyer sees rhyme as "the one string we have added to the Greek lyre": whereas "it enriches the harmonies of purely lyric poetry, and it makes verse easier to remember by heart," it "remains . . . an adornment and is not essential to poetry, as is demonstrated by the great body of our poetry that is written in blank verse."

Hillyer's conception of the role and the mission of the poet follows, likewise, from his view of the universe as an orderly and essentially benign entity:

A good poet is at home in his countryside and his world, and at one with the spirits and traditions of the past. These truths, however, are but aspects of the one truth that poetry is the highest expression of what is most natural to man in every phase of his life. The single idea of the poet is to create from disharmony, harmony; from formlessness, form. . . .

As an illustration, Hillyer says that "the majority of the modern poets" who give him "satisfaction," poets such as "Bridges, Frost, Robinson, Hodgson, . . . Yeats, Stephens and Gogarty, regard life, in spite of its dissonances, as essentially a harmony in which they are a part. They are at home in this world."

The posture of alienated romantic is very nearly a disqualification from poetry for Hillyer. His metaphor for the sensibility that brings harmony from dissonance is a Wordsworthian one, but instead of imaging the sensibility of an isolated and extraordinary individual, it images a communal sensibility, collectively attained:

The poet is the stained-glass window that transmits sunlight just as ordinary windows do, but colors it as it passes through. And the poet should rest content with that; no man is great enough to be both the window and the sunlight. And no man should be so perverse as to be merely a distorting glass.

Implicit in this figure is not only an appeal to tradition, but also the sense of a congregation to share that tradition. Perhaps this is the most enviable aspect of Hillyer's conception of poetry:

All art, in spite of many modern tendencies to the contrary, is more or less enduring as its intention is more or less communal, granted that the receptive community is the intelligent and responsive part of the general population. That is a minority and always has been.

Elsewhere, Hillyer remarks, rather poignantly:

There is so little reading of poetry nowadays. One reason for the decline of appreciation is the fact that poetry is so seldom read in family groups any more, or among teachers and pupils as a recreation rather than an assignment. And then, of course, so few people know how to read aloud.

The "decline of appreciation" which Hillyer remarks—the apparent end of a tradition in which a family might, instead of watching television, spend an evening reading aloud from Stevenson's *Home Book of Verse*—is nowhere more tersely described than in Edward Mendelson's introduction to *Early Auden*:

Among the historical crises faced, and, in part, invented by modernism was a breakdown in what might be called the symbolic contract, the common frame of reference and expectation that joins a poet with a finite audience, and joins both with the subjects of his poem.

Lionel Trilling is more explicit than Mendelson. He suggests that the debunking of the very communal kind of art that Hillyer defends was a deliberately conceived element of the cultural politics of the modernist overthrow:

Any historian of the literature of the modern age will take virtually for granted the adversary intention, the actually subversive intention, that characterizes modern writing—he will perceive its clear purpose of detaching the reader from the habits of thought and feeling that the larger culture imposes, of giving him a ground and a vantage point from which to judge and condemn, and perhaps revise, the culture that produced him.

Would any of today's really important poets in America accept Hillyer's comforting view of a metrical universe? Unlikely. But few of them, I suspect, would not envy Hillyer's premodernist image of the poetic vocation—of a world in which poetry enjoyed some general popularity, in which the poet could deploy with confidence a repertoire of fixed poetic forms. One cannot, of course, deny the desirability of many aspects of the modernist tradition. One need only open any copy of *Georgian Poetry* to observe that the rhetorical tradition against which the imagists reacted was far staler and more exhausted than Hillyer admits. Moreover, while the great modernist experiments were being conducted, it was inevitable that the experimenters see themselves as specialists, and it is no accident that the metaphor at the heart of Eliot's "Tradition and the Individual Talent" is drawn from chemistry: it required "scientists" to synthesize the new compounds, the new "art-emotions" that would replace the old. But the resulting losses were immense and have not yet been fully tallied. Just as Hillyer complained, the revolution has left the poet in America a bureaucratic specialist isolated in a university as in a laboratory, conducting endless experiments with poetic form, and in an adversary relation to the general culture.

*   *   *   *

Postmodern poetic form in American poetry is best understood as a reaction to the situation I have described; it is, however, variously also an attempt to recover, or at least pretend that there could now exist, favorable conditions analogous to those which Hillyer so intrepidly took for granted. Such form is not, as critics like Bloom would have us believe, Emersonian. That is to say, it is not "organic"; for Bloom's notion that a poem "ask the fact for form" is no more than the conventional organic theory of poetic form, a restatement, for example, of Denise Levertov's dictum that "form is never more than a *revelation* of content," a restatement in which Bloom has substituted "the fact" for "content." Perhaps oddly, the true notion of form which underlies our postmodern poetry, regardless of whether a given poem is in free verse or accentual-syllabic meter, is quite similar to Hillyer's premodernist conception of the "fixed forms." It refers to a category. When "form" is conceived and applied as a category in conjunction with the word "content," "content" must likewise be redefined so as to include more than some mysterious "feeling" revealed by "form." It must refer also to a category of subject matter.

But, it will be immediately objected, the form of most contemporary poems does not fit any known category. My answer to this is that our poems *do* fit formal categories— categories which poets are quite aware of but which, because the aesthetics of modernism has generated so much (often deliberate) mystification, have remained implicit. One of Allen Ginsberg's longest poems, for example, is called a "sutra." Some of Richard Hugo's poems are in the form of "letters." Much of William Stafford's poetry is a mimesis of conversation. Poets like Louise Glück or Carolyn Forché often resort to a kind of discourse, a "form" which in its details—rhetorical, prosodic, structural—resembles psychological and religious confession. Certainly some of Galway Kinnell's poems are attempts to imitate something like "primitive song," a sort of scream issuing not from a specific individual but from an archetypal, prehistoric human.

Whether it pretend to be a sutra, a letter, psychiatric confession, talk, primitive song, or whatnot, when a poem invokes some nonliterary analogue as a basis for its form, the name of the analogue becomes, in effect, the name of a category of form. To talk sensibly about postmodern poetic form, instead of resorting to vague, "organic" mystifications, we might better (1) recognize that postmodern poetic form is predominantly analogical; (2) extend the range of categories by which we refer to poems, using the analogues to name these categories. In fact, if an analogical poem is any good, the name of its formal "category" will tell us far more about the poem than even a term like "sonnet" or "villanelle." Consider the following poem by Gary Gildner:

First Practice

After the doctor checked to see
we weren't ruptured, _
the man with the short cigar took us
under the grade school,
where we went in case of attack
or storm, and said
he was Clifford Hill, he was
a man who believed dogs
ate dogs, he had once killed
for his country, and if
there were any girls present
for them to leave now.
                    No one
left. OK, he said, he said I take
that to mean you are hungry
men who hate to lose as much
as I do. OK. Then
he made two lines of us
facing each other,
and across the way, he said,
is the man you hate most
in the world,
and if we are to win
that title I want to see how.
But I don't want to see
any marks when you're dressed,
he said. He said, *Now*.

I suggest that the term "conversation" poem will tell us a great deal about "First Practice." It tells us that the author is speaking in his own person, directly to the reader. It tells us that, if the poem is going to be a successful mimesis of conversation, the prosody will have to seem relatively artless, yet be pronounced enough to lend the poem unity—be it blank verse or very skillful free verse. It tells us that the subject matter of the poem will be relatively quotidian, and that the poem's authority—what holds our interest in it and commands our respect—will have to come not, as in confession, from the speaker's unusual suffering, not, as in a mimesis of primitive song, from the grand claims of the unconscious, nor, as in the late-modernist metaphysical poem, from the speaker's literary expertise, but simply from the speaker's way of telling, the speaker's ethos, the speaker's sheer inventiveness (for this reason, the conversational analogue, though the most prevalent one in the early 1980s, is the most difficult one, because it places extreme demands on the speaker to be casually brilliant).

"First Practice," then, is, in form, a "conversation poem" whose subject matter is a reminiscence about junior-high football. Without the notion of an analogue, however, it is nearly impossible to describe this poem's form at all, let alone account for it. Is it a "lyric"? No, not in any conventional sense of that word, although it is around the length of a lyric, and its line length, though irregular, is about that of trimeter, a meter which Hillyer conventionally associates with "lyric." Because there is no category which will simply identify this poem, we must, in order to describe it, begin by enumerating its characteristics. It is narrative, in two stanzas, in the first-person singular, past tense; it is rather short, in free verse and in conversational diction. The more we list characteristics, the more we implicitly regard the poem's "form" in what Robert Pinsky would call a nominalist manner—not as a category but as a unique thing-in-itself—and are drawn toward an organic conception of the poem's form. Our analogical account of its form, however, is far more accurate (as well as economical) both as to the poem's intention and final result than an "organic" account could ever be, and the reason is simple. The very term "form" as Bloom deploys it or as organicists such as Levertov do acquires such a range of reference that it becomes meaningless.

*   *   *   *

A good example of the difficulties of the organic position is Denise Levertov's essay "Some Notes on Organic Form." Levertov begins as follows: "For me, back of the idea of organic form is the concept that there is a form in all things (and in our experience) which the poet can discover and reveal." She then suggests, mistakenly I think and in contradiction to Hillyer's notion of a "metrical universe," that "poets who use prescribed form" believe that "content, reality, experience is essentially fluid and must be given form" whereas poets "who look for new" forms have "this sense of seeking out inherent, though not immediately apparent, form":

A partial definition, then, of organic poetry might be that it is a method of apperception, i.e., of recognizing what we perceive, and is based on an intuition of an order, a form beyond forms, of which forms partake, and of which man's creative works are analogies, resemblances, natural allegories.

For Levertov, poetic composition happens as follows:

. . . first there must be an experience . . . or constellation of perceptions . . . felt by the poet intensely enough to demand of him their equivalence in words. . . . So—as the poet stands . . . contemplating his experience, there come to him the first words of the poem. . . . The pressure of demand and the meditation on its elements culminate in a moment of vision, of crystallization in which some inkling of the correspondence between those elements occurs; and it occurs as words.

According to Levertov, as the process of composition proceeds,

. . . content and form are in a state of dynamic interaction; the understanding of whether an experience is a linear sequence or a constellation raying out from and into a central focus or axis, for instance, is discoverable only in the work, not before it.

Levertov's account describes very accurately what composition in free verse feels like and the way in which the impact of a finished poem—its very life—requires that the poet "discover" something "in the work [of composition], not before it." But to refer to this impact, this feeling as if it were the *entire* "content" of a finished poem, and to refer to poetic "form" as if it were unconnected to any literary conventions or expectations whatsoever—as if "form" meant nothing other than "equivalence" to "an experience . . . or constellation of perceptions"—is not only seriously misleading but immediately leads to an impossible position. To see how this is so, consider the following description by Levertov of the "sonic" aspects of poetic composition:

Rhyme, chime, echo, reiteration: they . . . often are the very means, the sole means, by which the density of texture and the returning or circling of perception can be transmuted into language, apperceived. A may lead to E directly through B, C, and D; but if there then is the sharp remembrance or revisioning of A, this return must find its metric counterpart. It could do so by actual repetition of the words that spoke of A the first time. . . . Or it may be that since the return to A is now conditioned by the journey through B, C, and D, its words will not be a simple repetition but a variation. . . . Again, if B and D are of a complementary nature, then their thought- or feeling-rhyme may find its corresponding word-rhyme.

Levertov then summarizes all the specific formal possibilities so painstakingly enumerated above:

In organic poetry the metric movement, the measure, is the direct expression of the movement of perception. And the sounds, acting together with the measure, are a kind of extended onomatopoeia—i.e., they imitate not the sounds of an experience (which may well be soundless, or to which sounds contribute only incidentally)—but the feeling of an experience, its emotional tone or texture.

Levertov's argument exhibits much charm as well as admirable specificity. But it is this very specificity which reveals how meaningless such terms as "form" and "content" become when used in the drastically reductive sense that she uses them. If, as she implies, each experience were wholly unique, then each poem—which was the organic crystallization of an experience—would have a unique set of formal requirements for the expression of the "feeling" of that experience, requirements which could not be anticipated. There would be an *infinite* number of ways in which "A may lead to E." This is probably one reason why organicists invariably use the word "form" as a blank check that can refer to *any* element of a poem. In a good poem, there are too many factors at work to be spelled out. As a result, when Levertov claims that "form is never more than a *revelation* of content," she is arguing, in effect, that *every* detail of a poem's "form"—of its rhetoric, of its prosody, of its structure—contributes to its "content," i.e., the "feeling of an experience, its emotional tone or texture." But if we test any good poem against this claim, it simply does not stand up. Examining one of Levertov's poems, "Losing Track," a poem written around the time when she conceived "Some Notes on Organic Form," we see that although elements of its "form" *do* help "reveal" its "content," we can always discover arrangements of the poem which, though they may attenuate some of that feeling, do not substantially alter the poem's subject matter. Indeed, we begin to realize that "feeling" cannot exist without subject matter, without some context. The full "content" of a poem consists of both. We discover, in fact, that the "content" of this poem can be labeled:

Losing Track

Long after you have swung back
away from me
I think you are still with me:

you come in close to the shore
on the tide
and nudge me awake the way

a boat adrift nudges the pier:
am I a pier
half-in half-out of the water?

and in the pleasure of that communion
I lose track,
the moon I watch goes down, the

tide swings you away before
I know I'm
alone again long since,

mud sucking at gray and black
timbers of me,
a light growth of green dreams drying.

After the initial reading our attention is directed mainly toward the question of "content" with respect to the poem's subject matter rather than its content with respect to "feeling": we ask, "What is the poem about"? If the poem is the "crystallization" of an experience, what is the *type* of that experience? Implicit in this question is the assumption that each experience, although in many senses unique, may fit into a recognizable category; for indeed only to the extent that a poem admits the categorization of experience can it become a public rather than a wholly subjective utterance. With another reading, we conclude that "Losing Track" is about a love affair, the speaker's dazed paralysis, her helplessness, her enchantment by the intermittent sexual "communion" with "you," so that even when he is gone, she is preoccupied with him, passive: she waits for the tide to come in, the boat to return. But we also see that this "content" would be just as recognizable if the lineation of the verses were different, if the text were set as prose, if the stanza breaks were eliminated, if the order of the sentences were different, or even if some of the diction were changed. In other words, the poem's "content" is largely (though not entirely) independent of its "form."

No one, of course, would argue with Levertov that unless "the feeling of an experience" has, by some mysterious process, been transmuted into a poem's "form"—into its rhetoric, its prosody, its structure—the poem's verse format will seem to lack a raison d'être, and the resulting poem will be oddly lifeless. Nor would most people argue the fact that in Levertov's terms, "Losing Track" succeeds. Its archetypal imagery of "tides," "moon," and "water" evokes the depth of the speaker's awakened sexuality, which connects her physically, like a pier, to the earth, to the sea, to the rhythms of the universe, to the world's body. With its repeated vowel sounds, its line breaks that make the voice crack, make the breath catch in an almost sob, the poem moans and sings like blues. Indeed, we might be correct to say that in "Losing Track" "prosody is no more than a revelation of emotion." But to say that in this poem "form is *never more than* [my italics] a revelation of content" is to misrepresent it by focusing *exclusively* on the particularity of an experience and therefore treating the poem's "content" as if "content" consisted exclusively of ungeneralizable "feelings." More serious, it is to ignore the fact that a poem, even one in free verse, is first and foremost a convention, as indeed "Losing Track" reminds us. It is a lyric poem, observing all the decorum which we expect of that convention. In fact, it would not be too much to say that in this poem Levertov's very way of speaking—the speaker in solitude yet communing in public with somebody who is not present—is not merely dependent on the conventions of lyric: it is made *possible* by that convention.

*   *   *   *

As "Losing Track" suggests, viewed in relation to Levertov's organic theory, the notion of "organic form" in verse is most often associated with the lyric. Indeed, "organic form" might best be regarded as a sort of metaphor for the composite formal elements which make up the typical lyric, a type of poem which is the imitation of a recognizable, indeed almost conventional, kind of psychic process—a process that is nonrational, affective, intuitive, and (paradoxically) subverbal. The finished "organic" poem—the finished lyric—will therefore display the predictable tokens of such a process: it will often be in the present tense, in the "lyric" radical of presentation, with the speaker talking or musing to himself or herself; its prosody will probably be flexible; its overall shape will probably be rather plastic and its diction unstudied, a rhetoric of artful spontaneity.

Another good contemporary example of this type of poem would be Ted Kooser's "A Summer Night":

> At the end of the street
> a porch light is burning,
> showing the way. How simple,
> how perfect it seems: the darkness,
> the white house like a passage
> through summer and into
> a snowfield. Night after night,
> the lamp comes on at dusk,
> the end of the street
> stands open and white,
> and an old woman sits there
> tending the lonely gate.

As in the Levertov poem, because this poem's content consists of predominantly subverbal feelings, we find a heavy reliance upon imagery to evoke the unspoken, subliminal deathliness as well as the profound melancholy of the evening. Tone and emotion are not, as in Gildner's "First Practice," conveyed primarily by means of voice and line break but rather as they have to be, by means of imagery; for imagery, as Stanley Plumly has pointed out, is voiceless. It is this voicelessness, together with the countless past echoes that make up the lyric tradition, that gives the speakers of lyric their oddly generic quality.

"Lyric," then, like "conversation poem," is a category of poetic form, one that carries with it certain assumptions as to the nature of the speaker, type of subject matter, and type of rhetoric. Whereas Gildner's conversational analogue dictates a persona who is a particular (and rather ordinary) person, a quotidian subject matter, and a conversational rhetoric, the "lyric" category dictates a generic persona, a subverbal subject matter, and an organic rhetoric deploying a high degree of imagery. Indeed, it is as hard to imagine Kooser writing "A Summer Night" without sensing in advance what general type of poem he had in mind, as it is to imagine Gildner writing "First Practice" without having decided in advance to make his poem a mimesis of conversation. And it is in this sense that our poetry is still "fixed form." Analogues, each with its strictures as to decorum, have largely replaced the "fixed forms."

Literary form and literary convention have always been, of course, implicitly analogical. Indeed, every form of discourse alludes, in some sense, to every other form. But if we compare, for example, any of Richard Hugo's letter poems to Pope's so-called *Epistles*, we see that whereas in Pope's work the epistolary analogue is merely a framing device, within which most of the verse confidently proceeds in its heroic couplets as if oblivious of the fact that it is part of an "epistle" (indeed, much of Pope's *Epistle to Dr. Arbuthnot* is not like a letter at all but is in the form of a dramatic dialogue with "A."), Hugo's letter poems, in their intimate tone, in their vernacular diction, in their openings and closings, imitate the format of a personal letter far more consistently and with more care than Pope did. Conversely, if we look at the prosody of both poets, we notice that whereas Pope's heroic couplets are wrought with characteristic elegance, the Hugo letters are in a free verse so casual that it is scarcely distinguishable from prose.

Although a comparison between Pope's *Epistles* and Hugo's letter poems is only one of many possible such comparisons, it is, I think, an instructive one. The free-verse poem is much more dependent upon its analogue than is the fixed-form poem. Why? Because the poet writing in an accentual-syllabic prosody has a much clearer sense of how he is going to speak in advance; he has the assurance that his rhetoric will be, by definition, formalized by the prosody, be recognizably "poetry." The free-verse poet writing today, on the other hand, deprived of the comforts of convention, of the automatic chiming of an accentual-syllabic prosody, even though free verse has become normalized, still remains less certain than Pope was (or even Wordsworth was) about how to speak, how to sound when writing verse. It is in direct proportion to this lack of certainty that Hugo's reliance upon his letter analogue to guide the decorum of his rhetoric—to formalize it and organize it into a structure recognizable as art—increases. Whereas "premodernist" writers were able, I believe, to get the process of poetic composition underway by invoking an accentual-syllabic prosodic convention, the modernist and postmodern poet intuitively locates and then leans on some analogue or other as a springboard. The analogue may, of course, be changed in midstream—*The Waste Land*, for example, invokes various analogues; some of James Wright's later poems swerve from folksy conversation to deeply lyric passages of inwardly addressed meditation and back—but it is the initial invocation of analogue-as-convention which makes the poem possible in the first place, by suggesting a way of speaking.

This analogical basis for poetic form is what characterizes American modernist and postmodern poetry. Historically, it is apparent that whenever the raison d'être of "fixed forms" is in question, poets wistfully propound impossible "organic" notions of poetic form to replace the seemingly dead fixed forms, while instinctively reaching for nonliterary analogues as a fresh basis. The romantics, we recall, were attracted both to organicism and to analogical poetic forms: "conversation poems," precisely, or "lyrical ballads." Similarly, it is hardly an accident that Pound, wrestling in a later age with the amoebic growth of the *Cantos*, would invoke the analogies of "fugue" and "ideogram," that Eliot's *The Waste Land* invokes the collage as a formal analogy, that *The Four Quartets* invokes a musical analogy, or that *Paterson* would contain a high proportion of undigested, nonliterary material. Indeed, analogical poetic form may be regarded as a manifestation of a general literary principle: the further a poem deviates from fixed-form conventions and a traditional prosody, the more it will be compelled to seek, as a basis for its form, some nonliterary analogue. The self-evident quality of this principle may be appreciated if we reword it slightly. If a work of literature does not invoke, as the basis of its form, literary conventions, then, if it is to have a form, by definition that form will have to be nonliterary. Thus, for example, before the "novel" in English was sufficiently developed to be the name of a genre, it tended to be a mimesis of something else, such as journalism, romance, epistolary correspondence, spiritual autobiography. Thus it is that, in any epoch, in proportion to the degree that free verse becomes normalized, the analogues underlying poetic form tend to become nonliterary.

Just so, *postmodern* poetic form is *analogical* poetic form with a vengeance: though on the one hand it represents a refinement of the analogical approach to form implicit in poetry of the High Modernist period, on the other hand it evinces considerable dissatisfaction with the impersonality of modernism. Postmodern formal strategy consists, therefore, not only of extending the range of formal analogues, but also of clearly favoring "communal" analogues such as confession and conversation over such impersonal analogues as the "fugue," the "ideogram," and the "vortex." We can, in fact, order the prevalent formal analogues along a scale, to borrow Al Poulin's term, of their degree of "personalization." In the admittedly overschematic taxonomy that results, the outlines of three domains emerge distinctly and in a significant arrangement. Near the middle of this scale, we can locate and define a large, stable body consisting of a rather conservative type of poem that is "lyric"—a poem like Levertov's "Losing Track" or Kooser's "A Summer Night," spoken by a generic, literary "I" and deploying a traditionally "organic" rhetoric. The generic quality of the "lyric" voice may be regarded as an implicit norm, rejected on the one hand by modernists such as Pound and Eliot as being too personal, and modified, on the other hand, by such postmodern "confessional" poets as Lowell, Hugo, and Berryman so as to incorporate a broader, more particularized and more topical range of personal experience. To one side of the lyric norm, in the direction of greater personalization, may be located two types of poem— the "confessional" and, furthest from the center, the "conversational." The "confessional" poem, as its very name would imply, is a poem whose form is derived by analogy from the ritual of "confession," a ritual which in its religious aspect is Roman Catholic and in its secular aspect is psychoanalytic. It is a mimesis of testimony, in which the speaker either addresses the reader (often defiantly) or addresses some other person. The sense in which "confessional" may be regarded as a greater personalization of lyric may be appreciated if we imagine a blasphemous version of Keats's "Ode to a Nightingale" in which the speaker explicitly complained, in the first person, about his sexual needs, his medical and family problems, his *thanatos*. By particularizing the agenda of the inner life, placing its items in history and attributing psychological cause and effect to feelings—feelings traced back to specific origins, as elements of a unique autobiography—the speaker would lose much of his generic quality and, because the subject matter was no longer subverbal, would no longer be singing to himself but complaining aloud to a listener.

Whereas the authority of the lyric voice finds its source in tradition, the authority of the confessional voice finds its source in the authenticity of the speaker's testimony—a testimony which must, however, transcend the narrowly personal: to some extent, the persona's story must acquire, like a saint's life, a mythic significance. The persona must become a ritual scapegoat. Carolyn Forché's poem "Return" might serve as a paradigm of how, when the confessional analogue is successfully applied, the poem negotiates these paradoxical demands. The poem's journalistic "witnessing" for conditions in El Salvador has authenticity; yet for all the particularity of exposition, Forché is able, at the end of the poem, to convert her individual suffering into a prophetic stance:

> Your problem is not your life as it is
> in America, not that your hands, as you
> tell me, are tied to something. It is
> that you were born to an island of greed & grace
> where you have this sense of yourself
> as apart from others. It is not your right
> to feel powerless. Better people than you
> were powerless. You have not returned
> to your country, but to a life you never left.

Just as lyric modulates into confessional, so does confessional modulate into conversation. To the extent which the persona of confessional relinquishes the claim to mythic status and extraordinary suffering, he or she becomes further particularized. The conversation poem such as "First Practice" is at once the most personal and, because its subject matter is quotidian, the most difficult type of poem to write well. Its authority depends not on tradition or on authenticity but entirely upon the artistic inventiveness of the poet who, speaking in his or her own person, must sustain brilliant conversation. Gildner's "First Practice," a narrative conversation poem of voice, is a good paradigm of what Stanley Plumly has called "the prose lyric." To the degree that a conversation poem abandons narrative, it becomes discursive, modulating into the mode which it is now fashionable to call "meditative," a mode often shown to its best advantage by such poets as Marvin Bell, William Stafford, William Matthews, and Jorie Graham.

To the other side of the lyric norm, in the direction of impersonality, may be grouped respectively and in descending order of personalization those types of poems which, in various ways, elaborate and extend the modernist impulse to produce poems as objects which can exist independently of their author's implied biography. Immediately to the impersonal side may be placed what, for convenience, I will call "deep-image" poems. The deep-image mode, like the imagist movement fifty years before it, may be seen in part as a reaction against personalization in poetry, recalling, in its revulsion from confessional, T. E. Hulme's earlier dictum to the "romantic" poet to "End your moan and come away." The deep-image poem attempts to treat of the self, but of a self even more generic than the self implicit in lyric. The persona of the deep-image poem is, in fact, scarcely human. The three most prevalent analogues underlying deep-image poems are (1) that of a modern man screaming a prehistoric, primal scream; (2) that of a modern man dreaming in prehistoric symbols; (3) as some of W. S. Merwin's poems purport to be, that of the earth itself, speaking through the poet. All three of these analogues recall Galway Kinnell's well-known formulation: "If you could keep going deeper and deeper, you'd finally not be a person either; you'd be an animal; and if you kept going deeper and deeper, you'd be a blade of grass or ultimately perhaps a stone. And if a stone could read, poetry would speak for it."

Within the deep-image tradition, the same paradox that underlies lyric—that of rendering subverbal material by means of language—becomes increasingly acute the further we modulate from lyric in the direction of the inhuman. By far the best poetry in this tradition is by Kinnell—poems which, like "Under the Maud Moon," deploy what I would call "primitive song" as a formal analogue. The less human, the less personal the formal analogue, the weaker deep-image poetry becomes. Consider, for example, Robert Bly's "The Hermit," a poem which deploys archetypal dream-vision as its formal analogue and rather cavalierly asserts, through the pronoun "we," the universality of its vision.

> Darkness is falling through darkness,
> Falling from ledge
> To ledge.
> There is a man whose body is perfectly whole.
> He stands, the storm behind him,
> And the grass blades are leaping in the wind.
> Darkness is gathered in folds
> About his feet.
> He is no one. When we see
> Him, we grow calm,
> And sail on into the tunnels of joyful death.

Like a dream, the poem presents images. But whereas images in actual dreams have a powerful affect, a "numinosity" which according to Jung (Bly's model) is proportional to the charge of "psychic energy" which they carry, such images, dried out on the printed page, are reduced to abstractions. Because language alone cannot render the experience of numinosity, the poet tries, futilely, to tell us what to feel— "calm" and "joyful"—as we read.

The least successful formal analogue in the deep-image canon consists of the mimesis of the earth's "speech" itself, a wordless speech which is articulated verbally by the poem, with the poet, who does not appear directly, serving as a passive medium. Such a poem is W. S. Merwin's "Eyes of Summer":

> All the stones have been us
> and will be again
> as the sun touches them you can feel
> sun
> and remember waking with no face
> knowing that it was summer
> still
> when the witnesses
> day after day are blinded
> so that they will forget nothing

The vocabulary of the earth is elemental to the point of dullness. Translated into human words, it has the force of stale, romantic doctrine.

All three of the principal deep-image analogues, "primitive

song," "Jungian dream-vision," "Voice-of-Earth," deal with a single type of subject matter: they purport to put us back in direct touch with a primeval mode of consciousness. As all analogues do, these carry with them certain obvious requirements as to prosodic and rhetorical decorum. Primeval consciousness, approached directly instead of through the medium of civilized institutions, does not express itself by means of heroic couplets, or in a polysyllabic, abstract vocabulary, or in subordinate clauses, but through free verse, through what Paul Breslin has called "a studied plainness of vocabulary," through archetypal dream symbols, and through simple (in the case of Merwin's poem, deliberately suppressed) grammar. The decorum dictated by deep-image analogues is that of an organic rhetoric carried too often beyond the point of diminishing returns. Kinnell's "Under the Maud Moon" is successful precisely because it avoids the fallacy of imitative form. Instead of insisting on an innocence of vision commensurate with a primitive analogue, it accepts the paradox inherent in the very notion of rendering subverbal subject matter in language. It deploys the primitive-song analogue as a nostalgic but *sophisticated* commentary on the human Fall. Kinnell takes up his analogue longingly; but his best poems implicitly criticize the very analogue they are imitating. Consider, for example, the following passage from "Under the Maud Moon":

> The black
> wood reddens, the deathwatches inside
> begin running out of time, I can see
> the dead, crossed limbs
> longing again for the universe, I can hear
> in the wet wood the snap
> and re-snap of the same embrace being torn.
> The raindrops trying
> to put the fire out
> fall into it and are
> changed: the oath broken,
> the oath sworn between earth and water, flesh and spirit,
>   broken,
> to be sworn again,
> over and over, in the clouds, and to be broken again,
> over and over, on earth.

In this passage, Kinnell's attitude toward the purely physical world—that world which Bly and Merwin purport to accept without qualification—is far from comfortable. The speaker's longing for it is counterbalanced by fear of it, and his sense, hunched before the fire, of being in a starkly elemental position is counterbalanced by his clear consciousness of how far *outside* natural process (epitomized by the fire) he stands. Bly's "The Hermit" and Merwin's "Eyes of Summer," on the other hand, by taking too literally the epistemological demands inherent in their formal analogues, lack the tension generated by the necessarily paradoxical nature of achieved poetic form.

Continuing to extend our taxonomy, we may locate, contiguous with the deep-image category but in the direction of greater impersonality, poems whose forms are based upon what might be regarded as "literary" analogues: narrative poems such as Louis Simpson's Chekhovian pieces, in which the speaking voice resembles that of a novelist; dramatic monologues such as Robert Pack's recent work, in which the poet's voice vanishes altogether; and late-modernist "essay" poems such as Richard Wilbur's famous "Love Calls Us to the Things of This World," highly crafted pieces rich in literary diction and allusions, displaying conspicuous literary artifice, and spoken by a literary expert, a specialist. Whereas even in Merwin's "Eyes of Summer" the author retains a faint, vestigial presence as a character in his own poems, in the three types of poems above, the poet has removed himself fully as a character, and we are conscious of him only as a peripheral presence, as "The Author"; and it may be noted that, once an author has removed himself from his poem, the requirements regarding prosodic and rhetorical decorum are simplified. No longer does the speaking voice have to take into account such factors as the need to sound spontaneous, sincere, "authentic." The ethos of the author is no longer directly on trial or up for inspection. Whereas poems based upon nonliterary analogues present acute epistemological paradoxes—requirements for calculated spontaneity, for sophisticated primitivism, for mythologically resonant banal detail, for ordinary conversation with the force and staying power of art—the conventions associated with literary analogues render these modes of discourse far easier to manipulate without committing the fallacy of imitative form.

At the furthest end of the scale, absolute in their impersonality, may be grouped poems which are spoken by *nobody*, poems in which our sense even of the author's presence as a central consciousness all but disappears. These are poems in the so-called "postmodern*ist*" mode, for example, many of Ashbery's—poems which are asserted as objects and whose forms depend *entirely* upon analogues, in that they passively recapitulate all the possible modes of discourse, literary or otherwise. Such poems, placed beside the achieved conversation poem, reveal in stark outline the fundamental choice confronting the poet working in America today. It is a choice between analogues, between forms which, as we have seen, range from the communal to the impersonal. Curiously enough, this choice ends up being not an epistemological one but an ethical one, a test of an author's character and capacity: whether to trust one's vision and presume to impose upon the world, by sheer force of character, an individual aesthetic and ethical order, or to continue the modernist hegemony of Eliot and Pound, to retreat in an elitist disgust from modern civilization and indulge in the facile despair of the parodist, recapitulating all the bad languages that comprise our environment, holding our own civilization up before us as if the sad facts could only speak for themselves.

2. The Contemporary Conversation Poem

The most personal type of contemporary poem—personal because in this type of poem we find the poet speaking in his or her own person directly to the reader—is the poem which appropriates, as a formal analogue, ordinary conversation, the "conversation poem." But this mode, popular as it is, is also the most difficult mode.

As is true of all those kinds of poems which base their structure and rhetoric upon some nonliterary analogue—for example, upon religious/psychological confession, primitive song, or dream-vision—the conversation poem confronts the poet with two paradoxical demands. As with the confessional poem, the contradiction inherent in the conversation poem—a contradiction which ultimately determines the characteristics of the achieved conversation poem—centers on the authority of the speaking voice. The authority of the confessional voice finds its source in the authenticity of the speaker's testimony, a testimony which must satisfy two paradoxical requirements: it must provide sufficient journalistic detail so as to render a vivid historical sense of the speaker's past experiences; simultaneously, however, it must transcend the narrowly personal, so that the speaker's story acquires, like a saint's life, a mythic rather than a merely journalistic significance.

In the conversation poem, the problem of establishing the authority of the speaking voice is even more acute than in confessional. The speaker cannot lay claim to the ethical or moral authority of the confessional voice by virtue of testimony alone. Nor is the conversation poem a dramatic monologue. The reader must be willing to pay attention to a speaker about whom there is nothing inherently exotic or historically compelling. The speaker is not Bishop Blougram, the duke of Ferrara, or Jonathan Edwards. The speaker is no more than an ordinary man or woman speaking in his or her own person, sharing the same quotidian life as the reader. For the speaker to command our attention and respect, then, he or she must prove extraordinary by virtue of the very manner in which the poem is spoken. The conversation must be brilliant. The speaker must establish his or her own authority by means of art alone—a demand which points directly to the formal paradox inherent in the conversational analogue: how is one to produce a mimesis of conversation yet produce art, poems whose language resembles conversation yet is superior to it? For the conversation poem confronts us with a brutally clear criterion of critical judgment: if the poem on the page is not better than the best conversation, then it has no raison d'être. It becomes one more example of the fallacy of imitative form.

The conversation poem, then, recalls in many respects Wordsworth's conception of the poet as "a man speaking to men" and in "the language really used by men." But the contemporary conversation poem, which is postromantic, relies on a different conception of the poet. Whereas the Wordsworthian poet was endowed with "a greater knowledge of human nature, and a more comprehensive soul, than are supposed to be common among mankind" and with an "imagination" whose "colouring" he could "throw over . . . ordinary things" so as to reveal them "in an unusual aspect," the contemporary poet, bequeathed a poetic language in which Wordsworthian personifications are hackneyed and obsolete, must rely on totally different forms of invention in order to establish authority, an authority founded not on vision but on sensibility.

*   *   *   *

Although the term "conversation" includes many types of discourse, and the "conversation" poem appears in such diverse guises as the "poem of instruction" invented by Gary Snyder in his "Things To Do" poems, and in "letter" poems best exemplified by Richard Hugo's letter poems in *31 Letters and 13 Dreams*, we may distinguish two basic types of conversation poem, each with a characteristic kind of structure, diction, and prosody, suited to the type of conversation which is being imitated. The first type we might label "narrative." It is usually in free verse, and it comprises what might be labeled "the free-verse, narrative, conversation poem of voice," or what Stanley Plumly has accurately labeled "the prose lyric." The second type of conversation poem we might label "discursive," though the more fashionable term has come to be "meditative." In this type of poem, the conversation, instead of being anecdotal, tends to be digressive, abstract, and to include philosophical speculation; but its poetic decorum is apt to be significantly less formal than that of philosophical, late-modernist poems such as Richard Wilbur's vintage work, where conspicuous artifice renders unlikely any mimesis of conversation, and the absence of an "I" addressing the reader directly lends the poem a modernist impersonality, so that instead of being conversation directed to the reader by a person of similar background, the late-modernist metaphysical poem remains an elaborate art object synthesized by an elite specialist and handed down for study. Because meditative discourse assumes a greater degree of premeditation than narrative, however, the prosody of the meditative conversation poem admits a greater degree of formality than that of narrative conversation. Blank-verse cadences frequently crop up, and when they do, the meditative conversational mode invokes a style and tradition that leads back through Wallace Stevens to romantic conversation poems such as "Tintern Abbey." Each of the two main types of conversation poem seeks to establish the authority of the speaker's voice and sensibility in a different way. In the case of the narrative conversation poem, such authority, where it can be established, tends to be ethical authority, created by means of tone; in the case of the discursive conversation poem, the authority of the speaker tends to be aesthetic authority, established by the speaker's ability to manipulate analogies.

A good example of the fully achieved, narrative, free-verse conversation poem of voice is Susan Ludvigson's "Little Women":

> There in the playhouse
> making pies of flour and water
> and apples from the neighbor's yard,
> we learned to handle anything—
> husbands who stopped in
> just long enough
> to sample the cookies,
> gardens that washed away

in the first spring storm,
and babies crying,
their mechanical wails
stuck in their throats
like dimes. Sometimes
we thought we'd try something
else—I'd be
a missionary in Africa,
and a ballet dancer,
and go to Mars.
I remember standing on the sidewalk,
hands raised to the sky,
proclaiming *I* would not
be married, have children,
live in a neighborhood
like this. But always
we returned
to the little house
behind my real one,
put on the long dresses
with folds that wrapped us
like gifts,
the shiny high heels,
and the feathered hats.
Then we practiced
a dignified walk
around and around the block.

For this poem to work, the speaker must establish her ethos almost entirely through tone of voice. The poem stakes everything upon the complexity, the compassion, the moral authority of the speaking voice, which remembers a former innocence but neither sentimentalizes it nor rejects it—a voice which, at precisely those junctures in the poem where it could slip into bitterness or rage ("we learned to handle anything— . . . proclaiming *I* would not / be married" and the faintly comical ending), hits instead a gently sardonic and profoundly stoical note of humor, lending the poem its uninsistent but nevertheless pronounced aesthetic distance, its sense of the speaker's broad perspective, so that the poem judges without blaming and can manage, for all its sadness, not to refuse the world but to praise it.

The more closely we look at the poem's technique, the more we observe how its features are determined by the problems inherent in the conversational analogue. For example, the narrative conversation poem cannot indulge in flashy metaphors and similes, because to do so would not only interrupt the natural movement of narration but would also irreversibly ruin our trust in the ethos of the speaking voice. To see why, suppose that for "like dimes" we inserted some standard, contemporary, metaphorical formula such as "the adjective noun of noun": "their mechanical wails / stuck in their throats / like the bright slivers of dimes." By calling attention to itself as a piece of decoration, the metaphor would distract us from the story, from the voice, and call upon us to judge and approve the poet's ability to make a metaphor, her linguistic skill—an issue totally unrelated to the story at hand and which, once raised, would call into question the speaker's intentions: we would ask, is she trying to impress us, or is she concerned with her story? It is for precisely this reason that, in "Chapter and Verse," Stanley Plumly has argued that a rhetoric of "voice" and a "rhetoric of image" are, within the same poem, mutually exclusive tactics. But the incompatibility of decorative imagery with the narrative conversation poem leaves the poet with a seriously depleted assortment of means: it is free-verse prosody—the line break, the choice of line length, and the counterpointing of syntax against line— which brings into relief the drama of the story and the complex of emotions in the speaking voice as emotion is modified and enriched by the accumulation of context. This prosody is particularly effective in passages like "husbands who stopped in / just long enough / to sample the cookies," where the line breaks reproduce exactly the appropriately *knowing* tone of the voice: "*just* long enough," slight pause, then, with a tonal wink, "to sample the cookies." Another passage which could serve as a model of free-verse prosody in the service of "voice" would be:

> hands raised to the sky,
> proclaiming *I* would not
> be married, have children,
> live in a neighborhood
> like this. But always
> we returned
> to the little house
> behind my real one,

The line breaks, counterpointed against sentences, make the voice come down hard on "not" in the second line, and wearily on "always" in the fifth, whereupon the remaining three lines, by limply conforming to expected pauses, reinforce the sighing, slightly exhausted tone of resignation which ends the passage—a tone which, in the context of the poem's overall plot, acquires that subtlety of modulation, that highly civilized balance of irony, sadness, and humor, that is the peculiar forte of the free-verse poem of "voice," an effect which avoids extremes and risks preciocity but which can discriminate emotion, measure fine distinctions, and achieve an urbanity that accentual-syllabic prosody, with the slightly histrionic diction that goes with it, cannot.

Because the narrative conversational analogue limits to such an extreme degree the kind and the amount of literary artifice which the speaker can resort to without undermining the ethos of voice, poems in this mode constantly risk flatness, lapsing into prose. The opening three lines of the Ludvigson poem, for example, are dangerously flat, barely saved by the tonal tour de force of the fourth line and the passage that follows it. Not only do they lack rhythm, but they lack the alliteration, assonance, and rhyme which could bind them; they lack that density of sound which we do find at the end of the poem, where the rhythm and the touch rhymes are just pronounced enough to remind us that we are in the slightly intensified world of art.

The difficulty of sustaining such a balance between a mimesis of conversation on the one hand and art on the other is increased by the fact that, in today's literary climate, free verse has so nearly replaced the blank verse of Wordsworth's and Coleridge's "conversation" poems as "the language really used by men" that even blank verse has acquired a slightly literary, artificial sound. Because the decasyllabic cadence has been the cadence of such a vast proportion of earlier English-language poetry, the romantic "conversation" poem in blank verse must have been rather easier to write than "Little Women," for the cadence itself supplied the poet with a reasonably natural, ready-made verse frame in a language that was recognizably *poetry*. Indeed, if we look at the early dramatic poems of Robert Frost, such as "A Servant to Servants," we see that even as recently as fifty years ago, prosodic artifice did not have to be as carefully camouflaged as it is today in the narrative, free-verse poem of voice, where the decasyllabic cadence—any ten syllables within a syntactic unit ("their mechanical wails / stuck in their throats")—seems smuggled back into the verses as if to reassure us, subliminally, that we are hearing a formal utterance, and where rhymes—full rhymes and touch rhymes—when they cluster as the long *i* sounds, the consonant *d*, and the sound *and* do in the passage, "I remember standing on the sidewalk, / hands raised to the sky, / proclaiming *I* would not / be married, have children," must not do so in a way that looks too contrived.

Free verse is, of course, not the only prosody available to the narrative conversation poem of voice; but it is worth noting that, to the degree that the narrative conversation poem admits prosodic formality and imagery, it trades off tone of voice for other types of rhetoric. Such a trade-off—perhaps even a desirable one—is evident if we compare the Ludvigson poem to William Stafford's "Traveling Through the Dark":

> Traveling through the dark I found a deer
> dead on the edge of the Wilson River road.
> It is usually best to roll them into the canyon:
> that road is narrow; to swerve might make more dead.
>
> By glow of the tail-light I stumbled back of the car
> and stood by the heap, a doe, a recent killing;
> she had stiffened already, almost cold.
> I dragged her off; she was large in the belly.
>
> My fingers touching her side brought me the reason—
> her side was warm; her fawn lay there waiting,
> alive, still, never to be born.
> Beside that mountain road I hesitated.
>
> The car aimed ahead its lowered parking lights;
> Under the hood purred the steady engine.
> I stood in the glare of the warm exhaust turning red;
> around our group I could hear the wilderness listen.
>
> I thought hard for us all—my only swerving—
> then pushed her over the edge into the river.

In this poem some of the possibilities of voice have been sacrificed for the sake of formal beauty: the prosody is patterned, the lines are in four-stress accentuals and lightly dabbed with touch rhymes. The artifice, like the poem's conscious construction around the word "swerve," is unobtrusive yet constitutes a definite presence in our experience of the poem. The rules of the pattern leave Stafford enough flexibility to sound conversational, yet the poem manages, while sounding conversational, to remind us of poetry, one reason being that the accentual prosody as deployed here by Stafford contains so many buried echoes of traditional prosody. For example, the opening line consists of exactly ten syllables. Behind the strong-stress rhythm, we hear iambic pentameter. Most poems, in their very opening lines, declare their prosodic intentions in order to set up the reader's expectations so as to play off these expectations later in the poem, for special effects. When we run into other decasyllabic lines later in the poem—lines 7, 10, 14—and hit passages that have iambic phrasing, we begin to hear that the entire poem is playing two different prosodies in counterpoint, yet never obviously enough to seem artificial. Indeed, the best free verse does this, too—it is filled with echoes and resonances of traditional prosodies. Because of its ability to counterpoint and modulate between prosodies, to distill echoes, free verse, in the hands of a practitioner with a good ear, for example John Ashbery, is the ultimate prosodic instrument, infinitely more interesting and capable of musical complexity, infinitely more flexible than any one patterned prosody, but only so long as it is playing off of a traditional prosody. When it loses touch altogether with the tradition, it becomes no longer music but mere noise: prose.

*   *   *   *

The discursive, "meditative" conversation poem presents the poet with the same contradictory demands that the narrative conversation poem does; but because the requirement for an appearance of spontaneity is less than in the narrative mode, the contradictions inherent in the conversational mode are, in some respects, easier to negotiate than in narration. To observe how this is true, let us consider an example of the discursive conversation poem at its best, Jorie Graham's "For Hope":

For Hope

to continue and be
        gradually
different, it must
        be as free
as not, mechanical
        yet random,
a staggering
        forward.
Because we think,
        watching
the bluish spot a bird
        has just left,
where something's missing
        something
must be. And seen
        in this light
the boy now running
        past my open
window, holding a small
        model airplane
high over himself,
        is a glorious
machine. He's raging
        behind it,
squinting up into
        noonlight,
trying to feed it
        into the air,
into that other
        lawfullness
where it can ride
        on accident.
Meanwhile the late
        September day,
tired of returns,
        is leaning
in climbing vines
        over the stone,
is leaning in dust
        over the leaves,
dragging our crop in.
        The harvest
is the visible world,
        this boy

arms high above
                his head
running in sunlight,
                trying to turn desire
and an invented wind
                into an engine,
one that will pick up
                this pasteup
of paper and toothpicks
                and carry it way
past the natural. For hope
                to continue
and be gradually changed
                it must catch
accidentally
                on the draughts
of the impossible.
                Otherwise
who are the wise men
                bringing their gifts to?
Otherwise who is the man
                with his vast
catch of fish
                staring out at
from his photograph,
                or Apollo
in the painting by Antonio
                Pollaiuolo
with his hands on Daphne,
                holding her up
into the light, his prize,
                the only one
he ever wanted, as she
                continues
and is gradually
                lost?

We notice, first of all, that the relationship between speaker and reader in this poem is more casual than in the narrative poem. We are made explicitly aware of the time which the speaker takes out from talking directly to us in order to ruminate. It is as if the speaker were situated by her typewriter, by an open window, ruminating on "Hope," occasionally glancing out the window at the boy with the model airplane, then turning back to us to make an unhurried, somewhat studied comment. Because the decorum of this type of conversation admits of some premeditation—can be what William Stafford would call "considered speech"—the rhetoric of this discursive conversation poem, while it must remain offhanded enough to resemble conversation, can include more explicit artifice than the decorum of narrative allows. But the pressure upon the speaking voice to claim our attention is correspondingly more extreme. Whereas in the narrative conversation poem the admittedly ordinary persona of the speaker has an *occasion* for speech—a story that needs telling, that impels the speaker to action—the dramatic occasion behind the discursive conversation poem is minimal. It might be something which the speaker had read, or merely some vague, philosophical disquietude which he or she had wished to explore, to clarify. The charm of the speaking voice no longer derives from situation at all, but must be created entirely by the speaker—in the movement of her mind, its drift to invent, to play with analogies. Indeed, it would seem to be an almost self-evident principle: the less urgency in the "occasion" behind a given poem, the more the poem will, in order to establish a raison d'être, have to substitute its own capacity to conspicuously display artifice—either prosodic artifice or, in the case of the conversation poem, whose decorum discourages conspicuous musicality, development of arresting analogies. In fact, a comparison between the Ludvigson poem and the Graham poem suggests a second principle which is, perhaps, also self-evident: the less implicit metaphoric significance can be located in the occasion of a poem, the more a poem will tend to feature an explicit display of analogy-making. Except for "like dimes," "Little Women" contains no explicit analogies; but the entire playhouse world as regarded by the speaker is an implicit metaphor for her complex attitude toward the fact of having been born and raised a female. The main incident behind "For Hope," on the other hand—a boy with his plane outside the window—has only as much significance as the poet can make of it. Hence the entire poem consists of pure extrapolation, is built on analogies: the boy's hope that the glider will fly parallels the desire of the poet's eye to possess the departed blue spot of the bluebird which, in turn, parallels the speaker's wish that her own words, like the plane, catch on inspiration, "on the draughts / of the impossible" and so be carried "past the natural." It is almost inevitable that the achieved discursive conversation poem be self-reflexive, to acknowledge, as it must, the self-created occasion by which it brought itself to birth—brilliant conversation created for its own sake, flying under its own power, like all achieved art, on "draughts of the impossible," on pure, daring suspension of disbelief. At its best, the "meditative" conversation poem stays aloft this way, like Frost's "Birches" or, in its more urbane decorum, like so many of the later poems of Stevens—the mind formulating its serious, playful constructions, flying itself with theorems, telling us over and over again that without this play, without words to stay the light "leaning in dust," our loss would be absolute.

3. Pinsky's *The Situation of Poetry* and Imagistic Convention

The late 1970s, beginning with Robert Pinsky's *The Situation of Poetry* (Princeton University Press, 1976), saw a gush of brilliant, opinionated "practical" criticism. Close on the heels of Pinsky's book followed Stanley Plumly's important two-part essay, "Chapter and Verse," published in *The American Poetry Review* (1977), Paul Breslin's dissection of the mindlessness and complacency of "deep-image" rhetoric and poetic convention, "How to Read the New Contemporary Poem" (*The American Scholar*, 1978), and C. O. Hartman's study of prosody, *Free Verse* (Princeton University Press, 1980), a book which in its sensitive, detailed explications of poems was implicitly opposed to deep-image convention and to its announced ontology. More recent books such as Robert Hass's *Twentieth Century Pleasures* (Ecco, 1984) continue to elaborate the reaction against what the eminent critic Charles Altieri has labeled "a poetics of immediate experience" predominant in the late sixties and early seventies. But Pinsky's book remains the seminal document in this critical movement, a book which, in retrospect, reveals, under its meticulously scholarly veneer and its rigorously modulated tone, some of the qualities of a manifesto. Fifty years from now, this manifesto may be recognized as equivalent in influence and historic significance to such documents as Pound's "A Few Don'ts," to T. E. Hulme's "Romanticism and Classicism," to any of the venerable "imagiste" manifestos studied in Modern Poetry classes today.

Indeed, if we compare Pinsky's manifesto with those of the *Imagistes*, we can find some remarkable ironies. Pinsky is arguing for a readmission to poetry of some of the very discursiveness and possibilities of abstract discourse which the imagists, starting around 1913, had attempted publicly to ban. Pinsky's position is two-fold: (1) he argues that because language is by nature "abstract," poetry can accommodate ideas and abstract discourse far more readily than many poets and critics believe; (2) he questions the still-common assumption that one of the primary tasks of a poem is to render sensory experience by means of "images"—to "show" and not "tell"—tracing this assumption back through Pound and the modernists to the romantics.

Perhaps even more ironic than this turning against itself of literary taste and the inevitable appearance of a truly influential anti-imagist manifesto is that Pinsky's manifesto, a manifesto which is intellectually and stylistically far superior to the original *Imagiste* and "Amygist" manifestos, employs tactics to discredit "imagistic" poetry that are similar to the tactics which the original architects of imagism used to discredit Victorian poetic convention. Instead of appealing to the reader's taste, Pinsky, like Pound and Hulme, resorts to epistemological arguments. Pinsky's argument is much more closely reasoned than those of Hulme and Pound. But, like all philosophical arguments adduced to justify a poem or a poetic style, this one is not up to the job. One cannot redeem a poem or a poetic style by means of extrinsic argument. Poetry must do the job alone.

In the best extant book on the imagist movement, *In the Arresting Eye: The Rhetoric of Imagism* (Louisiana State University Press, 1980), John Gage compares imagist poems to imagist manifestos to determine whether the poems actually carry out the aesthetic and epistemological programs set forth in the manifestos, programs epitomized by such old saws as "direct treatment of the thing." Gage demonstrates, at times wittily, how seldom imagist poetic practice followed its own theory. Gage concludes that "theory," for all its philosophical clamor, was mainly an attempt to educate the taste of the English and American reader of that time to a different type of rhetoric, to train readers steeped in threadbare Victorian rhetoric—"luxurious riot," as Pound termed it—to an unfamiliar convention. Convention, not epistemology, was the real issue.

Pinsky's "manifesto" is similar. It is an attempt, using the rhetorical authority of philosophical argument, to influence literary taste, to call into question conventions which, most observers of American poetry would agree, had grown stale, complacent. As we might expect, the *positive* elements of

Pinsky's position—his demand for the inclusion of more abstract statement in poetic discourse—are persuasive, their
plausibility almost self-evident. Most of Pinsky's specific complaints about poems are justified, too. He is impatient with
the tendency of contemporary poets to insist on the freshness
of their observations by stocking poems with deliberately startling and strained metaphors and similes; and he is indignant
at the complacency of MacLeish's dictum, "A poem must not
mean / But be." But the epistemological argument which he
musters to condemn complacently used imagist conventions
and rhetoric is so sweeping that it condemns, under the title
of "the nominalist poem," *any* contemporary poem, no matter
how good, which, written in the present tense and containing
a high proportion of physical description and imagery, would
seem to render the immediate feel of a particular experience.
The *argument*—not Pinsky's taste, which is reliable and is
borne out irrefutably by his own beautiful poems—Pinsky's
argument fails, and the failure of this argument is instructive;
for the argument itself, as I will presently demonstrate, inherently misrepresents poetic convention. It cannot acknowledge that, in the evolution of poetic form, convention has
priority over epistemology.

The basic assumptions behind Pinsky's point of view he announces immediately in his introduction:

The premises of their [the modernist poets'] work included a mis-
trust of abstraction and statement . . . and an ambition to grasp
the fluid, absolutely particular life of the physical world by using
the static, general medium of language. Those premises are paradoxical, or at the least, peculiar, in themselves. Moreover, the brilliant
stylistic inventions associated with the premises—notably the tech-
niques of "imagism," which convey the powerful illusion that a poet
presents, rather than tells about, a sensory experience—are also peculiar as technique.

Or, they once seemed peculiar. These special, perhaps even tor-
mented premises and ways of writing have become a tradition: a
climate of implicit expectation and tacit knowledge.

These premises, Pinsky maintains, constitute "the common
roots of two varying and familiar contemporary styles," both
of which "seem to base themselves upon some of the same
grounds: prominently, a dissatisfaction with the abstract, discursive, and conventional nature of words as a medium for
the particulars of experience." The "two styles" which Pinsky

then describes are roughly equivalent to the two rhetorical strategies—(1) the "silent" rhetoric of "image"; (2) the "rhetoric of voice" characterizing "the prose lyric"—which, independently from Pinsky, the poet/critic Stanley Plumly arrives at in his ground-breaking essay "Chapter and Verse." The main difference between Plumly's distinction between two "rhetorics" and Pinsky's distinction between "two . . . contemporary styles" is that whereas Plumly emphasizes the ways in which narration and "voice" have adapted themselves to free verse, Pinsky restricts the issue almost entirely to that of poetic diction, the issue of abstract discourse versus imagistic "discourse":

That dissatisfaction may be expressed by pursuit of the physical image purified of statement, or in other instances by pursuit of an "allegation" purified of imagistic eloquence. In either case, the dissatisfaction is ultimately insoluble because of the nature of words and verses.

As an example of "the physical image purified of statement," Pinsky adduces one of Robert Creeley's better pieces, a stripped-down love poem oddly reminiscent of "Western Wind":

> Could write of fucking—
> rather its instant or the slow
> longing at times of its approach—
>
> how the young man desires,
> how, older, it is never known
> but, familiar, comes to be so.
>
> How your breasts, love,
> fall in a rhythm also familiar,
> neither tired nor so young they
>
> push forward. I hate the metaphors.
> I want you. I am still alone,
> but want you with me.

The poem displays, Pinsky says, "a winning and useful directness," even though it is "neither convincing as naturalistic speech nor persuasive as sharp physical description." The poem *is* "winning"; but Pinsky's subsequent comment is a bit puzzling. Never mind that the poem is in the form of a letter—that it was never intended as a mimesis either of "naturalistic speech" or of some moment of consciousness in the poet. Why raise the issue of mimesis in the first place? Why even hint that that issue could or should be applied to the business of practical criticism, of judging the quality of a poem? We are fairly sure, for example, that hawks do not speak or think in English. Should we therefore never try to imagine what a hawk might think or say if hawks had language? Should a poem never presume to speak for elements of the world that are inhuman, inarticulate? Does a poem like Ted Hughes's "Hawk Roosting" because it presumes to attribute thoughts in English to a bird therefore fail? Yet it is just this kind of epistemological issue which, throughout his essay, Pinsky invokes to call into question the imagistic poetry which he finds "naive" and lacking in "statement."

The heart of Pinsky's critique is his third and central chapter, "The Romantic Persistence," much of which is a detailed and fascinating explication of Keats's "Ode to a Nightingale," focusing on the limitations of poetry—of language in general—to render experience accurately. As Pinsky puts it:

> If what one loves and wishes to approach is embodied by unconscious being, . . then the very calling of poetry is a problem. Every word is an abstraction, the opposite of a sensory particular; sentences are abstract arrangements, and the rhythms of verse like all rhythms are based on the principle of recurrence, or form.

> For these reasons, Keats can move . . only *toward* the Lethe of the bird or the landscape. Though he seems later in the poem to arrive there, what I see as the firm moral base of the poem rejects that idea. . . . In Keats' terms, his fancy cannot quite delude him that it is possible to cross over, making his poetry into something as purely phenomenal and undeliberate as the nightingale's song. His painstakingly artful stanzas, his inventive diction, his unsettling awareness of time, prevent him from joining that unutterable realm. The very words he uses, because they are the most conscious part of him, recall his isolation from the landscape into which the bird so easily fades. . . . Can the poet's words about the world so unlike himself approach the objectivity of vision, or do they present only a waking dream?

This quandary, Pinsky says, is reflected in contemporary poetry by the "pressure to avoid or camouflage statement and abstraction" and in "the extraordinary refinement of so-called 'free' verse" which "can be seen as part of a flight from abstraction or recurrence, a pursuit of the status of a thing, a unique moment in time." Pinsky then rests his case with the following passage:

Strictly speaking, the ultimate goal of the nominalist poem is logically impossible. Language is absolutely abstract, a web of concepts and patterns; and if one believes experience to consist of unique, ungeneralizable moments, then the gap between language and experience is absolute. But the pursuit of the goal, or the effort to make the gap seem less than absolute, has produced some of the most remarkable and moving poetry in the language. Naturally, it has produced much dross, too. My proposition is that the difference between the dross and vulgarization on the one hand, and genuine work on the other, is a sense of cost, misgiving, difficulty.

The remainder of Pinsky's book consists of testing various texts against this criterion, in order to separate the dross from the genuine. And, from the preceding argument, one can easily guess that, for Pinsky, the difference between dross and good poetry is the degree to which a poem will admit abstract statement, will supplement its imagery with "statement," will, in short, use language in a manner consonant with its abstract nature.

It is tempting to object to Pinsky's argument on the same grounds that one might object to his critique of the Creeley poem—that epistemological issues are simply irrelevant to the quality of poems, which are, after all, fiction made possible by conventions which are blatantly artificial. But even if we grant the pertinence of epistemological requirements to literary judgment, we find that their very assumptions lead to serious contradiction. The most fundamental equivocation on which Pinsky's premise rests is the casual way in which he refers, on the one hand, to "that unutterable world" and, on the other hand, to "experience" that consists "of unique, ungeneralizable moments." As he puts it: "The numberless particular fragments of nature, each different, are also numberless instants in time, each unique and without reference to what comes before or after." What Pinsky wants to describe here is "perception" as it might be to Keats's inhuman nightingale. But then he says: "It is the poet's nature to organize these separate paradises, in effect contaminating them with his awareness of sequence, sentence, rhyme, connections of all kinds."

It is easy enough to agree with Pinsky that the elements of

the natural world are so Other as to be "unutterable" except in human terms. One might also agree with Pinsky that, for a nightingale, perception consists of "numberless instants in time, each unique and without reference"; but when he talks about the poet's "contaminating" paradises, he is clearly talking about *human* "instants in time," human experience; and he is trying to suggest that raw human perception, unorganized by poetry—by the imposition of language at all—is as absolute as the nightingale's. The reason for this equivocation seems apparent: in order to maintain that the abstract nature of language makes it impossible for language to render human experience accurately, one must keep to this exaggerated position. But Pinsky's conception of nonverbal human experience is incredible. Even if we grant, for purposes of argument, that he is right—that, strictly speaking, each moment of a person's perception is unique—it would seem virtually self-evident that most "moments" of human experience *are* referential, that we intuitively recognize, if only at a subverbal level, affinities between different "moments," that the many feelings of familiarity which we experience—a familiarity that is actually a form of meaning (e.g., "It is going to snow")—be it recognition of a face, a street, a mood, a smell, or a profound sense of déjà vu, are not *imposed* upon the world by language: they are endemic to human experience, which is filled with "sensory experiences" and "images" which are analogical, mutually referential. In other words, imagery is, in itself, a kind of language. Obviously, it is not the only language, nor is it the only language of poetry; but surely a poet's tendency to deploy images is more than a "romantic persistence" or, as Pinsky would have it, a tired leaning upon the modernist distrust of abstraction and statement. The mustering of images is a rather natural way, I think, of trying to clarify the flux and mess of experience, to achieve a momentary stay against confusion.

A good example of a superior poem which relies on this referential aspect of imagery, leaning more heavily on images than Pinsky might find acceptable, is Galway Kinnell's beautiful "Getting the Mail":

> I walk back
> toward the frog pond, carrying
> the one letter, a few wavy lines

crossing the stamp: tongue-streaks
from the glue
and spittle beneath: my sign.

The frogs'
eyes bulge toward the visible, suddenly
an alderfly glitters past, declining
to die: her third giant step
into the world.

And touching
the name stretched over the letter
like a blindfold, I wonder,
what did *getting warm* used to mean? And tear

open the words,
to the far-off, serene
groans of a cow
a farmer is milking in the August dusk
and the Kyrie of a chainsaw drifting down off Wheelock
    Mountain.

Never mind, for a moment, that this poem, even though it is
in the present tense, does not attempt to present an experience directly, that if it did—if the speaker purported to be
thinking aloud—the words "I wonder" would be stricken
from the third stanza. Let us assume that the poem is, as
Pinsky would put it, more "naive" than it is, that it *is* trying
to present experience directly. Two questions present themselves. First, despite the absence of explicit "statement," does
the poem make a statement? If so, could this statement be
made more effectively in more abstract language, by being
more explicit?

A moment ago, I suggested that imagery constituted a kind
of language in itself. The first stanza of the Kinnell poem ex-
emplifies well the evocative and referential nature of images.
The strong sense of the solitude of the speaker; the intrusion
of the "one" letter, which, with its tongue-streaks and "spittle," exerts an effect upon him almost as strong as the warm
physical presence of a person; the raw, wet, fleshly associa-
tions of ponds, frogs, spittle, and tongue combine to evoke a
slight feeling of physical suffocation in the speaker, a sense
(frequent in Kinnell's poetry) of his unease in the physical
universe, the sense of a minor yet disconcerting threat to his
being, as if he were on the threshold of vision. This sense of

the speaker's poise at the precipitous edge of vision is intensified in the second stanza, which presents a complex of contrasts: that of the wet, fleshly frogs against the dry, glittering light; the fly in range of the frog's tongue; the minute tolerances that define flesh from thought, light from darkness, the living from the dead; all these tensions heightened by the word "declining," which contains the paradox that to choose life is to choose to die. With just a couple of strokes, the stanza evokes a raw, physical sense of the contingency of all these aspects of existence. The frog's tongue recalls the tongue-streaks on the letter, and the "step into the world" of the alderfly recalls the "I walk" of the first line, drawing the reader further into the wet contingency of the physical world that is both the speaker's body and its environment.

In the third stanza, as the speaker balances on this edge of awareness, holding the letter, half-savoring the suspense before opening it, the letter seems to throw his entire existence into relief. He recalls how he felt as a child when, blindfolded, he would hunt for something and be told he was "getting warmer" the closer he came to the target. He knows that he is on the verge of a secret.

In the fourth stanza, as he rips open the letter and in effect touches the person who wrote it, he breaks the pressure of his solitude, he experiences a wave of relief as he is suddenly brought into communion with his surroundings, as if by opening and touching the Otherness of the person who sent the letter he has brought his being into closer relation with his immediate physical surroundings. As the poem ends, he experiences a sublime moment of calm, of reassurance, of connectedness with the world, of ease with his own physical life, as if he had just been suddenly unblindfolded, able to see for miles (as the frogs cannot), able to rejoice in Being, even though Being entails "declining to die," as though dying were merely the third "step into the world." The "serene groans" of the cow, in pain from its milk, dependent on the milker, who is in turn dependent on the cow; the sound of the chainsaw cutting dead wood for fuel to keep a man warm and alive: these images evoke the contingency of existence, a contingency which was, a moment ago, menacing but which the speaker can now intuit to be so in the nature of things that for a moment the sound of the cow and the saw are the song of existence itself, as it dies and births—a hymn.

This movement from psychic apprehension through a threshold into what Stanley Kunitz has called, referring to Roethke's poetry, "the rebirth archetype," is familiar to most of us, both in our experience and in literature. Roethke's "The Lost Son" describes such a curve, as does, in a more jagged curve of greater amplitude, Lowell's "Skunk Hour." This psychic process is, I would maintain, recognizable enough to constitute a "statement." Moreover, as my labored explication should demonstrate, the subject matter that makes up this statement is subtle enough that it has to be evoked delicately, by the most indirect means: its articulation *requires* the language of imagery. But does the poem, as Pinsky would wish, convey a sense of "the cost, misgiving, difficulty" of using language to capture this kind of experience? No. Nowhere does Kinnell, like Keats, abstractly philosophize on the difficulty of finding words for the experience. Yet the experience which the poem describes feels authentic and recalls to us our own precarious states of being.

Perhaps the most telling limitation in Pinsky's epistemological argument, however, is that, inherently, it cannot comprehend the convention of present-tense narration. It confuses the apparent immediacy furnished by writing in the present tense with the apparent immediacy which, Pinsky alleges, images try to evoke. A good example of how this confusion comes about may be seen in Pinsky's discussion of the following passage of poetry by Robert Bly:

> I am driving; it is dusk; Minnesota.
> The stubble field catches the last growth of sun.
> The soybeans are breathing on all sides.
> Old men are sitting before their houses on carseats
> In the small towns. I am happy,
> The moon rising above the turkey sheds.

This passage is an example, Pinsky says, of what happens "when a poet proceeds as though such illusions were not the final products of art, but the principles of art, starting points—then the result is precious, self-consciously and elaborately 'direct.'"

Pinsky goes on to attack the tone of the passage, saying that it "drifts from uncertainty into boastfulness, a kind of more-imagistic-than-thou attitude," and he is right about the qual-

ity of the poetry here. It is bad, but not for the reasons which
he alleges. Although what bothers him about the passage is
its tone, he attacks the tone on epistemological grounds—on
the grounds of the passage's purported "directness," unable
to acknowledge that in this passage the present tense does *not*
imply a complacent philosophical posture but is nothing
more than a narrative convention. When a contemporary poet
writes in the present tense, he does not do so in order to
assert that what he is describing is happening "right now" or
to assert the kind of "naive" directness and immediacy to
which Pinsky quite validly objects. Rather, present-tense narration is a convention implying a set of rhetorical possibilities,
an attitude by the speaker toward the *past* experience which
he is reenacting in the present tense. As in all first-person
narration, in the Bly poem we find dramatic irony. The author
knows more than the "I" of his story and has decided, by
writing in the present tense, to evoke the sense of wonder
and inner excitement which the "I" had once felt, at dusk, in
Minnesota. Indeed, if we compare the Keats with the Bly passage, we see that the Keats poem is far *more* naive than the Bly
passage, that Keats strives for a much greater degree of immediacy than Bly does. "Ode to a Nightingale" would put us *into*
the poet's mind so that we might feel and suffer with him, so
that we might lose all consciousness of the poet as narrator
talking *to* us. By means of its expletives, the poem strains time
and again to assert an absolute immediacy of the very kind
that Pinsky distrusts: "O for a draught of vintage! . . . O for a
beaker of the warm South!" Such expressions, intended to be
taken as sheer moans, deny any aesthetic distance between
the poet and his poem or his audience.

In the Bly passage, on the other hand, when the speaker
says "I am happy," he deploys the "I" in order to *distance* himself, the author, from "I," the protagonist, to try for an ironic
glimpse of that "I" in the midst of life. Just as in Bly's famous
little poem "In a Train," where the speaker announces, "I
have awakened in Missoula, Montana, utterly happy," we
sense in the passage above a certain amusement, a certain
astonishment, a certain ironic attitude on the part of the
speaker at the way in which these odd "moments" of hap-
piness manifest themselves when you least expect them. As
in the Kinnell passage, we see the poet reenacting a scene in

which he is the protagonist, all the time quite conscious that the scene is a *re*enactment, and making no attempt to conceal the resulting aesthetic distance.

The present tense is the tense of "reenactment," a workable literary convention establishing a limited but definite aesthetic distance between author and "I," between now and then, such that the reader can watch the narrator watching himself. Both the reader and Bly know, as well as Pinsky does, that no literature can present human experience directly.

Just how conscious poets are of the conventions of narrative may be suggested by the fact that Louis Simpson has entitled an entire book of poems *Adventures of the Letter I*; and indeed the reader may get some idea of how *any* epistemological argument such as Pinsky's tends inherently to misrepresent the convention of contemporary present-tense narration if we look closely at a Simpson poem which, like the Kinnell poem, would seem at first glance to be complacently "direct," without "statement":

> After Midnight
>
> The dark streets are deserted
> With only a drugstore glowing
> Softly, like a sleeping body;
>
> With one white, naked bulb
> In the back, that shines
> On suicides and abortions.
>
> Who lives in these dark houses?
> I am suddenly aware
> I might live here myself.
>
> The garage man returns
> And puts the change in my hand,
> Counting the singles carefully.

In this poem, the "I," having perhaps stopped for gas, finds himself, a member of the upper-middle class (signified by his melodramatic fantasies of drug-store suicides and the infantile expression "garage man"), in a neighborhood that is somehow sinister. At the end of the poem, he experiences a feeling of relief when he receives his change and can drive away. The poem is preeminently about money, about the poet's consciousness of how he and members of his socioeconomic class pay their way through life, about how strangely thin the line can seem between those who live "in these dark houses" and where "I myself" live—the difference of a few greasy bills in the back pocket. The poem thus dramatizes an incident in which the "I" is led to an uneasy moment when those bills are the only things *physically* protecting him from life on the other side of the line. But how much of this does the "I" know? Far less than Simpson, the poet. Simpson is grimly watching somebody like himself, as that person comes into knowledge. At the end of the poem, the protagonist, "I," is simply relieved. But the *narrator*, Simpson, who understands the meaning of the narrative, who has in fact contrived it, and who feels connected (as he is) to the protagonist, is chagrined and critical of both himself *and* the "I." The poem thus clarifies a complex moment of ethical self-consciousness in the narrator, by *pretending* to present experience directly and immediately. For the poem to assert greater aesthetic distance between the poet and the "I"—for example, to be cast in the past tense—would destroy the way in which the poem actually dramatizes the shock of dawning ethical self-consciousness, because it would eliminate the slight but *deliberate* confusion which the poem establishes between its narrator and the "I"; for it is through this confusion that the reader actually experiences the chagrin of self-knowledge as he realizes that the poem is *criticizing* the "I"—the very "I" with whom the reader, by convention, initially identifies himself.

"After Midnight" is a tremendously sophisticated and successful poem. Although it makes no explicit statements, the implicit statement dramatized by the poem as a whole is devastating. Indeed, this "statement" could not have been made this accurately by any other means. That an epistemological argument lacks the terms by which to deal with a poem like this one is, I think, a stunning example of the way in which systematic Theory, applied to literature, tends to ruin it, ensnaring the critical intelligence in approaches which, because they refuse to acknowledge that literature is defined primarily be convention, because they refuse to acknowledge that convention is *not* reasonable but exists through a shared suspension of disbelief, end up denying the complex, paradoxical experience of poetry as it was and still is meant to be experienced by a sophisticated reader.

4. The Abstract Image

Two related strands of poetic diction have been handed down to contemporary American poetry from a tradition which we might label roughly "surrealist." The first of these strands, predominantly Spanish in origin and one which we might label "archetypal," has been brilliantly analyzed and criticized by Paul Breslin in his essay "Nihilistic Decorum in Contemporary Poetry,"[1] where he states:

> . . . a narrow and dull decorum has spread over most, though not all, poetry in America. Its characteristics include a studied plainness of vocabulary and syntax, a reliance on hackneyed "archetypal" symbols, and an eclectic, sentimental primitivism.

Breslin goes on to say:

> . . . predictable in a poetry of archetype, is the codification of language into a generic vocabulary. In describing the same object, one may choose from a range of nouns extending from the most general ("stone") to the most specific ("topaz"); one can be still more specific by adding modifiers ("this four-carat smokey topaz"). Both ends of the spectrum have their uses, but if one cleaves always to the generic, the result is a stylization of imagery, analogous to highly stylized forms of art.

In *The Situation of Poetry*, Robert Pinsky describes this type of archetypal diction in the following terms:

> One of the most contemporary strains in contemporary poetry is often interior, submerged, free-playing, elusive, more fresh than earnest, more eager to surprise than to tell. The "surrealist" diction associated with such writing sometimes suggests . . . a *particular* reality, hermetically primitive, based on a new poetic diction:

---

1. This was the title of the essay delivered by Breslin at MLA, which was later, in a version with a milder tone, published in *The American Scholar* as "How to Read the New Contemporary Poem." The quotations here are from the original essay, which was more sharply polemical in tone than the final published version, and, in my opinion, slightly better.

"breath," "snow," "future," "blood," "silence," "eats," "water" and most of all "light" doing the wildly unexpected.

It is this strand which has been associated with the "deep image" (the "generic image" would be a more accurate label) and which, as both Breslin and Pinsky demonstrate, has been worked to the point of exhaustion.

The other strand of contemporary poetic diction, one deriving mainly from the French surrealist tradition, has not received the attention which the "archetypal" strand has, perhaps because, until quite recently, it has not been so widely adopted. This strand utilizes a highly abstract diction in propositions which, instead of presenting generic images, make abstract philosophical generalizations, statements which, despite their *absolute* level of generalization, exhibit a peculiar epistemological invulnerability. The poetry of John Ashbery is the chief witness for this strand of surrealist diction, for example, "A Tone Poem":

> It is no longer night. But there is a sameness
> Of intention, all the same, in the ways
> We address it, rude
> Color of what an amazing world,
> As it goes flat, or rubs off, and this
> Is a marvel, we think, and are careful not to go past it.

> But it is the same thing we are all seeing,
> Our world. Go after it,
> Go get it boy, says the man holding the stick.
> Eat, says the hunger, and we plunge blindly in again,
> Into the chamber behind the thought.
> We can hear it, even think it, but can't get disentangled
> from our brains.
> Here, I am holding the winning ticket. Over here.
> But it is all the same color again, as though the climate
> Dyed everything the same color. It's more practical,
> Yet the landscape, those billboards, age as rapidly as before.

Typical of the kind of abstract generalizations which characterize this second strand of surrealist diction are passages like "We address it, rude / Color of what an amazing world, / As it goes flat, or rubs off." This type of proposition, which combines an extreme level of abstraction ("Color," "world," "it") with such concrete expressions as "rubs off," has received comparatively little critical discussion. The most thorough (though rather unsystematic) analysis of it is by Gene Frumkin, in his essay "The Reason of Surrealism" in *Chelsea* (1979). Much of Frumkin's discussion adduces as its prime witness for "the reason of surrealism" a Robert Bly translation of Pablo Neruda's "Sonata and Destructions," a poem which exhibits both strands of the surrealist diction that I have distinguished.

Sonata and Destructions

After so many things, after so many hazy miles,
not sure which kingdom it is, not knowing the terrain,
traveling with pitiful hopes,
and lying companions, and suspicious dreams,
I love the firmness that still survives in my eyes,
I hear my heart beating as if I were riding a horse,
I bite the sleeping fire and the ruined salt,
and at night, when the darkness is thick, and morning
      furtive,
I imagine I am the one keeping watch on the far shore
of the encampments, the traveler armed with his sterile
      defenses,
caught between growing shadows
and shivering wings, and my arm made of stone protects me.

There's a confused altar among the sciences of tears,
and in my twilight meditations with no perfume,
and in my deserted sleeping rooms where the moon lives,
and the spiders that belong to me, and the destructions I am
      fond of,
I love my own lost self, my faulty stuff,
my silver wound, and my eternal loss.
The damp grapes burned, and their funereal water
is still flickering, is still with us,
and the sterile inheritance, and the treacherous home.
Who performed a ceremony of ashes?

Who loved the lost thing, who sheltered the last thing of all?
The father's bone, the dead ship's timber,
and his own end, his flight,
his melancholy power, his god that had bad luck?

I lie in wait, then, for what is not alive and what is
      suffering,
and the extraordinary testimony I bring forward,
with brutal efficiency and written down in the ashes,
is the form of oblivion that I prefer,

the name I give to the earth, the value of my dreams,
the endless abundance which I distribute
with my wintry eyes, every day this world goes on.

The "archetypal" strand of diction is evident in such images as the "sleeping fire," "darkness," "wings," and "stone." The second strand may be seen in such sentences as "Who loved the lost thing, who sheltered the last thing of all?" and "the extraordinary testimony I bring forward, / . . . is the form of oblivion that I prefer, / the name I give to the earth, the value of my dreams, / the endless abundance which I distribute / with my wintry eyes." Frumkin does not distinguish between these two strands of poetic diction when he says of the poem, " 'Sonata and Destructions' blends its elements within a subterranean superstructure so effectively that its abstractions become particular, its specifics general, its extremes natural and its final evocation powerful." But the strand of surrealist diction which converts "specifics" to the "general" is, of course, the archetypal one; and the strand which manages to make "abstractions . . . particular" is the Ashberian one. The abstract nouns such as "things," "terrain," and "firmness" have, in the context of Neruda's poem, an oddly particular quality. So pronounced is this quality that, as we drift in the poem's spell, we forget that, except for a vague, dank, interior, crepuscular atmosphere, there is no clear "scene" that we can envision. The propositions themselves suffice as a kind of imagery. Even though the passage above is extremely abstract, we take it almost as description.

Intimately related to this "descriptive" quality exhibited by the poem's abstract propositions is what Frumkin calls their lack of "distilled information." As he puts it, the poem "harbors . . . surprising turns of speech . . . , some of which might be paraphrased easily enough while others could be approached exegetically only with trepidation, if at all." Frumkin then goes on to remark, correctly I think:

The main problem Surrealism has had in the literary community is that the typical poem in this vein—or the poem which is an alloy of surrealism and something else—is not altogether susceptible to those exegetical standards we have, to whatever extent, grown familiar with in the pre-postmodern era. The Anglo-American critical vocabularies are based, after all, on the necessity, even the priority, of overt conceptual ordering.

But this exegetical difficulty, which Frumkin sees as part of the surrealist tradition, is really not a characteristic of the "archetypal" strand—dreams can, after all, be interpreted—but rather of the second, what I have been calling "Ashberian," strand. When we encounter a sentence like Ashbery's "We plunge blindly in again, / Into the chamber behind the thought," or, in the Neruda poem, "There's a confused altar among the sciences of tears," even though each of these propositions advances a sweeping generality, we have no strong inclination to test its truth or falsity or to translate it into some other terms. We feel that these propositions embody a kind of figurative truth that is its own testimony. This semantic opacity is perhaps best suggested by Philip Wheelwright's term "Assertorial Lightness," defined in Wheelwright's words as quoted by Frumkin: "The reluctance of a poetic statement to be meant with full logical and epistemological rigor, together with its claim of being yet somehow meaningful."

To get a better idea of how this kind of proposition operates, let us examine some in detail. Take, for example, the opening of the second stanza of Ashbery's "A Tone Poem": "But it is the same thing we are all seeing, / Our world. Go after it, / Go get it boy, says the man holding the stick. / Eat, says the hunger, and we plunge blindly in again, / Into the chamber behind the thought." What gives this type of discourse, despite the apparently daring breadth of its generalizations ("It is the same thing we are all seeing"), its oddly unimpeachable epistemological quality is a peculiar mixture of the abstract and the concrete. In the first two lines, "the same thing we are all seeing," "Our world," and "it" (of "Go after it") have an almost endless range of reference. In fact, the "it" of "Go after it" need not refer to "Our world"; it can refer to anything. In context, however, the existence of "Our world" as a possible antecedent invites the reader to take "it" more seriously than if "it" were merely the end of the idiom, "Go after it." "It," then, assumes a certain epistemological value while retaining the widest range of reference possible. Its abstractness is absolute. Paradoxically, however, the expression "Go after it" has strongly concrete overtones: we imagine a man throwing a stick to a dog. These concrete overtones, reinforced by the context of the passage, are what make us suspend possible disbelief in the generalization. We are not inclined to test it or the previous proposition, "it is the same thing we are all seeing, / Our world." Instead, the concrete overtones of "Go after it" induce us to take the entire passage as an image rather than a statement; and an image, after all, purports to do no more than simply present an experience and let that experience speak for itself.

A simpler example of this type of abstract proposition, of a generalization which functions like an image—the "abstract image," it might be termed—is the passage directly below the one we have been analyzing: "and we plunge blindly in again, / Into the chamber behind the thought." Here again we find a proposition that invokes simultaneously two kinds of epistemological convention. The concrete overtones of "plunge blindly in" give the sentence the logic of an image—of physical description intended to speak for itself—yet the abstract quality of "the chamber behind the thought," enhanced by the definite articles, together with the "we," which emphasizes the range of the proposition, gives it the quality of a generalization. It may be objected that this type of proposition is confused, that it combines the abstract and the concrete in precisely the way that Pound warns against when he counsels writers to avoid expressions such as "dim lands of peace." There is, however, a difference, I think, between "we plunge blindly in again, / Into the chamber behind the thought" and "dim lands of peace." Whereas in the former, the element of concreteness is borne by the predicate, the staleness which Pound sees in "dim lands of peace" derives from the staleness of its syntactical formula—adjective noun of noun—whose concreteness is borne primarily by "dim" and whose abstract noun has, in context, a sentimental usage. How such formulas as "dim lands of peace" exhaust themselves is beautifully summarized by Northrop Frye in his *Anatomy of Criticism*:

In all ages of poetry the fusion of the concrete and the abstract . . . has been a central feature of poetic imagery in every genre, and the kenning has had a long line of descent. In the fifteenth century we have "aureate diction," the use of abstract terms in poetry, then thought of as "colors" of rhetoric. When such words were new and the ideas represented by them exciting, aureate diction must have sounded far less dull and bumbling than it generally does to us, and have had much more of the sense of intellectual precision that we feel in such phrases as Eliot's "piaculative pence" or Auden's "cerebrotonic Cato." The seventeenth century gave us the conceit or intellectualized image of "metaphysical" poetry, typically Baroque in its ability to express an exuberant sense of design combined with a witty and paradoxical sense of the stress and tension underlying the design. The eighteenth century showed its respect for the categorizing power of abstract thought in its poetic diction, in which fish appear as the finny tribe. In the low mimetic period a growing prejudice against convention made poets less aware of the conventional phrases they used, but the technical problems of poetical imagery did not thereby disappear, nor did conventional figures of speech.

Two of these connected with the matter under discussion, the fusion of the concrete with the abstract, may be noted. An abstract noun in the possessive case followed by an adjective and a concrete noun . . . is a nineteenth century favorite. . . . In the twentieth century it was succeeded in favor by another phrase of the "adjective noun of noun" type, in which the first noun is usually concrete and the second abstract. Thus: "the pale dawn of longing," "the broken collar-bone of silence," . . . on examining a volume of twentieth-century lyrics I find, counting all the variants, thirty-eight phrases of this type in the first five poems.

*   *   *   *

Although it is surely the poetry of John Ashbery that, more than any other work, has normalized the abstract image in the current literary milieu, whereas Ashbery's mature work consists of poems built almost entirely of abstract propositions, in the works of some of our younger contemporary poets we see the tactic of the abstract image deployed in more conventional contexts. Take, for example, the following poem by Jorie Graham:

Jackpot

Halfway through Illinois on the radio
they are giving away jackpots.
I can hear them squeal as they win.
Luck in this landscape lies flat
as if to enter the ground and add to it as well.
You can see its traces, milkweed caught in the fences,
the sheen on the new grass
that could be sunshine or white paint.
But the brushstroke is visible.
We wouldn't believe anything we saw without it—

the brown, the green, the rectangle, the overpass.
I believe now that sorrow
is our presence in this by default.
In a little while I hope there will be shadows,
the houses and these trees trying to bury half of themselves.
This could be your lucky day,
the day the roof is put on the house,
and the willows once again resemble trees,
and the bridge falls in, making the river once again
sufficiently hard to cross.

Here, in line four, the word "light"—the word we would expect—has been replaced by the more abstract "luck," which
is then elaborated by the concrete-sounding predicate "lies
flat." "You can see its traces, milkweed caught in the fences, /
the sheen on the new grass / that could be sunshine or white
paint" identifies "luck" with a peculiar quality of light; but the
full force of "luck" suggests more. It suggests the overall
quality of the landscape—what it is the fate or "luck" of the
landscape to be. "Luck in this landscape lies flat / as if to enter
the ground and add to it as well" suggests the blandness, the
lack of aspiration, the implacable prima facie aspect of this
place, seen from the monotony of an interstate highway "halfway through Illinois." It is the "luck" of this place to be ab-
sorbed in its own banality, to lie "flat" in every sense of that
word; moreover, in the context of the AM radio quiz show the
passage suggests that the surrounding human culture is as
oppressively "flat" as the land. The speaker's almost claus-
trophobic discomfort with her situation is expressed precisely
in the understated line—a beautiful, realistic deployment of
the abstract image technique—"I believe now that sorrow / is
our presence in this by default." The pronoun "this" has all
the ambiguity of an Ashbery pronoun: its range of reference
is nearly endless, referring at once to the speaker's position in
Illinois, in a car, in a culture which gabbles about meaningless
jackpots, as well as to "this" world, "this" moment of total
alienation from the surrounding landscape outside the numb-
ing monotony of the car, to the absolute "this" that is simply
the given. The term "our presence" carries both an abstract
and a concrete meaning. The abstract sense of "our presence"
suggests "our" being in the "present" moment: our existence.
The concrete visual sense of the phrase suggests our physical
"presence" in "this" spatial setting. Thus we may observe

that, in spite of the sentence's degree of abstraction, despite its apparent explicitness and its rather dry, flat tone, it functions both as an image and as an abstract proposition. It fuses idea—an explicit criticism of the banal world of jackpots and flatness—with emotion: "Sorrow . . . by default" is a strictly modulated metaphor for the speaker's discomfort—a feeling implicit and complex enough to resist easy paraphrase. We notice, also, that the abstract image permits a kind of emotional complexity—an urbanity—which the deep image does not, that the abstract image is not, as the deep is, limited to what Breslin has called a "psychological pastoral":

The determination to speak from the unconscious carries with it a set of pieties and avoidances, designed to purify the poet from the distractions and contaminations of the superficial and merely conscious. . . . The result is the latest permutation of the pastoral ideal, which has always praised the simple, calm, and spontaneous life, away from the vain complexities of cities and courts, and has often had a didactic purpose. Ours is a psychological pastoral. Just as Europe in the fourteenth century, according to Huizinga, turned to the pastoral idyll out of weariness with the complex and unrealistic demands of the chivalric ethos, American poetry has turned to an idealized and simple version of the psyche out of weariness with many things.

A good example of this psychological pastoral—how it holds forth a simplified, schematic version of the world—would be Robert Bly's "Surprised by Evening":

> There is an unknown dust that is near us,
> Waves breaking on shores just over the hill,
> Trees full of birds that we have never seen,
> Nets drawn down with dark fish.
>
> The evening arrives; we look up and it is there,
> It has come through the nets of the stars,
> Through the tissues of the grass,
> Walking quiet over the asylums of the waters.
>
> The day shall never end, we think:
> We have hair that seems born for the daylight;
> But, at last, the quiet waters of the night will rise,
> And our skin shall see far off, as it does under water.

In its generic vocabulary, which features "dust," "shores," "hill," "trees," "birds," "fish," "stars," "grass," and so on, we see a relatively extreme example of the kind of codification of language which Breslin and Pinsky have so well defined. We notice also that, like virtually all of that poetry which relies heavily on archetypal diction, this poem holds forth an essentially romantic vision: that underneath the phenomenal world associated with light and day and land, underneath the visible garment of Nature ("hill," "grass"), there resides a deeper reality associated with "darkness" and "water." Indeed, in the codified diction of archetypal poetry, the words "darkness" and "the dark" have become conventional metaphors for an invisible reality that cannot be seen by the eye but can only be apprehended by the imagination or through the lens of dream.

The poetic of the abstract image, on the other hand, tends to be compatible with a realist view of things, to admit and even to celebrate complexity, paradox. Jorie Graham's "Jackpot," although its ending yields to the longing for a culture less dependent upon technology, does not, like the Bly poem, content itself with an easy denial of the efficacy of things as they are. Rather, it deploys the tactic of the abstract image in order to arrive at and to clarify a difficult accommodation to the given: "I believe now that sorrow / is our presence in this by default." Indeed, in some recent poems the conspicuous deployment of the abstract image would seem to constitute an explicit denial of the dualism we seen in archetypal poetry like Bly's. As Ashbery's "A Tone Poem" rather pointedly puts it: "It is no longer night. But there is a sameness / Of intention, all the same, in the ways / We address it." And later: "But it is the same thing we are all seeing, / Our world. . . . We can hear it, even think it, but can't get disentangled from our brains." Similarly, in the passage "We plunge blindly in again, / Into the chamber behind the thought," Ashbery is describing the attempt to apprehend some possible reality behind the appearances of things; but unlike the Bly poem, here the penetration of mind and language into the color of the world yields only the discovery that "it is all the same color again."

Another poem—one formulated explicitly to deny, by means of the abstract image, the soft romanticism of archetypes—is Robert Hass's "Transparent Garments":

> Because it is neither easy nor difficult,
> because the outer dark is not passport

nor is the inner dark, the horror
held in memory as talisman. Not to go in
stupidly holding out dark as some
wrong promise of fidelity, but to go in
as one can, empty or worshipping.
White, as a proposition. Not leprous
by easy association or painfully radiant.
Or maybe that, yes, maybe painfully.
To go into that. As: I am walking the city
and there is the whiteness of the houses,
little cubes of it bleaching in the sunlight,
luminous with attritions of light, the failure
of matter in the steadiness of light,
a purification, not burning away,
nothing so violent, something clearer
that stings and stings and is then
past pain or this slow levitation of joy.
And to emerge, where the juniper
is simply juniper and there is the smell
of new shingle, a power saw outside
and inside a woman in the bath,
a scent of lemon and a drift of song,
a heartfelt imitation of Bessie Smith.
The given, as in given up
or given out, as in testimony.

Like the Ashbery poem, Hass's poem describes a movement of the mind as the mind goes "in" to the world. As the mind begins this journey, it is apt to be encumbered with dualist, romantic superstitions, to be "holding out dark" as "promise of fidelity," as that invisible reality (either inner or "outer") which one might worship either as "passport" to some deeper truth or with too much awe, with "horror." What the mind may discover, however, is that, as Ashbery puts it, "It is all the same color" (in Hass's poem, "White"), that the world is "clearer," that "juniper / is simply juniper," that the world is "The given." The title, "Transparent Garments," like so much of the phrasing in the mode of the abstract image, has an almost unlimited metaphorical range of reference. In context, it seems to allude heavily to the idea of the phenomenal world as a "garment" (the metaphor harks back immediately to its ultimate development in Carlyle's *Sartor Resartus*) cloaking an invisible noumenal world. It seems also to allude to the body and to "matter" which, "purified" "in the steadiness of light," becomes something "clearer." "To emerge" is thus to discover that, for all intents and purposes, the difference between inner and outer, between what is under the garment and the garment itself, is insignificant. Hence, as Hass's poem expresses it, the garment of the physical world is, for all practical purposes ("It's more practical," says Ashbery), transparent, concealing no "unknown dust," no "waves breaking on shores just over the hill," no "quiet waters of the night."

Both the Hass poem and the Ashbery poem reject the romanticism associated with the deep image in favor of the urbane realism of abstraction; yet the tactic of the abstract image is motivated by many of the same factors which once made the archetypal mode so appealing—by the desire of postmodern poets to flee the limits of confessional, the limits of the poem as personal testimony, and yet to construct a poetry that treats of the self. As both Donald Hall and Paul Breslin have pointed out, one of the chief attractions of the archetypal mode has been its inherent capacity to convincingly assert generalities. Writing in 1971, Hall praised the "movement" which Breslin later finds "hackneyed" as a way out of the limits of confessional:

The movement which seems to me *new* is subjective but not autobiographical. It reveals through images not particular pain but general subjective life. This universal subjective corresponds to the old objective life of shared experiences and knowledge.

Breslin, writing from the vantage point of greater hindsight, remarks, "It [the 'decorum' of 'archetypal' poetry] has to do with a reaction against confessional poetry, and with a new desire for universality and aesthetic distance."

The abstract image, which manages to generalize the observations of the single self ("I believe now that sorrow / is *our* [my italics] presence in this by default") without risking the tests which most generalizations invite, enables a poet to speak personally, out of his own life, yet to preserve that sense of generality which serious literature demands. It is also, I think, a more rhetorically convincing method of asserting generality and achieving aesthetic distance than is the rather cosmetic tactic of converting the "I" of a poem to "you" and thereby insisting adventitiously upon the general relevance of reported experience that may be particular and personal to the point of triviality.

The appeal of the abstract image is, however, more than rhetorical. If we reexamine the Ashbery and the Hass poems, we notice that neither poem is dependent, as is the dramatic lyric, upon the rendering of a conventional "scene" with a protagonist. In this latter type of conventionally descriptive poetry, for example in Robert Frost's "Stopping by Woods on a Snowy Evening," the burden of the "action," as in a realistic short story, is borne by the protagonist (who is often the poet himself), and much of the poem's energy is dependent upon the poem's dramatic situation being sufficient to keep the protagonist moving, changing, reflecting. Indeed, one reason why it is comparatively easy to write poems which describe physical action—chopping wood, playing baseball, hiking— is that the brunt of the physical exertion, borne mainly by verbs, can be translated directly and naturally into the poem's medium, its language. But even if the resulting poem is vivid and bristling with energy, its text—the written record of a particular experience—competes implicitly with the experience itself. One might say that the actual occasion behind the poem "Stopping by Woods on a Snowy Evening" threatens to make the poem about it secondary. A poem like Ashbery's "A Tone Poem," on the other hand, assumes value primarily as a thing-in-itself precisely because it is not set in one-to-one correspondence with a particular experience as referent. Thus the action in the poem, instead of taking place in the mind of an imagined persona responding to a particular situation, may take place almost entirely *within* the language of the poem. Indeed, one might say that the protagonist of the poem *is* its propositions.[2]

A related feature of the abstract image—one which may make it increasingly attractive to poets—is that abstract statement permits a far wider range of subject matter than we generally find in a poem dependent entirely upon occasion. The emotional range, the subject matter of poems based upon a particular "occasion"—on a dramatic situation or incident—is necessarily limited, because such poems tend to seek their

2. In his recent book *The Transparent Lyric* (Princeton University Press, 1984), David Walker finds frequent examples of this kind of poem, which he labels "the transparent lyric," in the poems of William Carlos Williams and Wallace Stevens. In Walker's formulation, the protagonist of these poems becomes "the reader."

own justification in their occasion and therefore to seek moments of emotional or visionary intensity stemming from a particular event. As a result, the type of event they treat is apt to fall into the category of the unusual.

In a poetry that allows full play to abstract statement, however, a poem can generate itself out of its own language. Like philosophical discourse, it can find its raison d'être through the formulation of something like an argument. When a poem is not based upon any particular occasion—upon the relatively infrequent events in a person's life that are intense—instead of being restricted to a narrative or testimonial character, it can adopt a discursive, "meditative" character; and when we encounter such poems, we can see that it is this type of discourse, with its fusion of the abstract and the concrete, that the genre of verse has traditionally seemed most adapted to framing, that our lingering modernist biases, expressed in the cliché "Show, don't tell," point directly to a dead end: poetry as mere description.

But one of the most attractive aspects of poetry has always been its capacity for pithy, epigrammatical generalization. Even in a fairly descriptive, image-rich poetry—for example, the poetry of Robert Frost—the finest moments are apt to exhibit a high degree of abstraction and explicit generality.[3] Indeed, it may be that the language of poetry is ultimately distinguishable from the language of prose not by its imagery or its rhythm but rather by this epigrammatical quality—its ability to survive in the valley of its saying, to climb hand over hand, phrase after phrase, from one ear-catching rung of distilled experience to the next, as William Matthews, displaying the abstract image to its maximum advantage and beauty, does at the conclusion of "Long":

>   . . . If the dead complained
> they would say we summon them poorly,
>
> dull music and thin wine, nor love
> enough for the many we make,
> much less for the melted dead
> in their boxes. Above them
> we talk big, since the place is vast

3. For example: "I craved strong sweets, but those / Seemed strong when I was young; / The petal of the rose / It was that stung."

and bland if we tire of looking closely,
washed bland by light from what light
lets us see, our study,
the scripture of matter,
our long narcosis of parting.

II

The Live Form

Criticism and formulations of criticism are the coral
reefs of literature, but the live part doesn't have a name.
And the live form is what's happening in the immediacy
of composition.

— William Stafford

5. Poetry and Commitment

Toward the end of her harrowing account of political repression in El Salvador, an account published in the July/August 1981 issue of the *American Poetry Review*, the poet Carolyn Forché raises several literary issues traditionally associated with "political" poetry, issues which in the context not only of her testimony but also of our current right-wing political milieu take on a particular urgency. Forché writes:

All poetry is both pure and engaged, in the sense that it is made of language, but it is also art. Any theory which takes one half of the social-esthetic dynamic and accentuates it too much results in a breakdown. Stress of purity generates a feeble estheticism that fails, in its beauty, to communicate. On the other hand, propagandistic hack-work has no independent life as poetry. What matters is not whether a poem is political, but the quality of its engagement.

"Engagement," with its French, existentialist echo, is itself a loaded word; but in the context above its usage becomes rather more ambiguous than necessary. Engagement with what? With political facts? With the process of composition? As we read further, we begin to suspect that Forché's vagueness of usage is deliberate, particularly when we come to the following passage:

There is no such thing as non-political poetry. The time, however, to determine what those politics will be is not the moment of taking pen to paper, but during the whole of one's life. We are responsible for the quality of our vision, we have a say in the shaping of our sensibility. In the many thousand daily choices we make, we create ourselves and the voice with which we speak and work.

Although Forché is careful not to spell it out, the aim of her argument becomes apparent. If the term "engagement" refers to a person's *political* involvements, and if there is no poetry that is "non-political," then "quality of engagement," like "the quality of our vision," is simply Forché's euphemism for the "quality" of a poet's ideological stance; and therefore when Forché argues that the quality of a poem ("What matters") is dependent on the "quality of its engagement," she is, in effect, suggesting that ideology *does* matter in a poem, that a necessary (but not, perhaps, sufficient) condition for a poem to be of high quality is that it evince a high degree of commitment. As any examination of Anglo-American "committed" poetry over the last fifty years will show, however, including some of the poems in Forché's own *The Country Between Us*, she is wrong. It is precisely when the distinction between what is political and what is not breaks down or is denied that the quality of art declines.

What happens to a poet when he or she can no longer distinguish between the political and the nonpolitical—why committed poetry is so difficult to write—may be seen in some of Forché's own work. Following the conclusion of her *APR* essay, where she calls for a "poetry of witness," we are treated to her poem "Ourselves or Nothing." Presumably an example of the "poetry of witness," the poem is a long, agitated, personal commiseration addressed to Terence Des Pres. After detailing her wonderment at Des Pres's moral staying power, she describes some of the experiences in El Salvador which have enabled her to understand at the gut level what Des Pres had meant in

> the pained note
> where ten times you had written
> the word *recalcitrance* and once:
> you *will die and live*
> *under the name of someone*
> *who has actually died.*

The poem ends:

> There is a cyclone fence between
> ourselves and the slaughter and behind it
> we hover in a calm protected world like
> netted fish, exactly like netted fish.
> It is either the beginning or the end
> of the world, and the choice is ourselves
> or nothing.

This ending, which recalls the desperate "We must love one another or die" in Auden's "September 1, 1939" (before he deleted it), has the hysterical note we hear so often in the utterances of poets who have been hurt by history and witnessed firsthand its implacable indifference to individuals. Indeed, it is a note which goes back to the French segment of Wordsworth's *Prelude*, and a note which we find in all committed poetry that has been written under the immediate stress of history. Such poetry exhibits two main characteristics. First, its vision is such that there is no detail of life without political meaning, as if observed in the glare of a terrible religious fixation, the very kind of fixated vision which causes Forché to exclaim, "There is no such thing as non-political poetry." It is this same fixation which in Auden's "Spain 1937" threatens to reduce the meaning of every quotidian human transaction to something significant only in terms of abstract historical factors:

> . . . "Our day is our loss. O show us
> History the operator, the
> Organizer, Time the refreshing river."
>
> And the nations combine each cry, invoking the life
> That shapes the individual belly and orders
> The private nocturnal terror:
> . . . .
> And the life, if it answers at all, replies from the heart
> And the eyes and the lungs, from the shops and the squares
> of the city:
> "O no, I am not the Mover,
> Not today, not to you. To you I'm the
>
> "Yes-man, the bar-companion, the easily-duped:
> I am whatever you do; I am your vow to be
> Good, your humorous story;
> I am your business voice; I am your marriage."

The second salient characteristic of any highly topical (nonsatiric), committed poetry—a characteristic which, likewise, may be observed in those parts of *The Prelude* dealing with the French Revolution—is a sense of baffled pain, accompanied by complaints about the banality of political activism and the thanklessness of the work and how exhausting it is. Part and parcel of these complaints is the poet's loss of confidence in not only the usefulness of his or her own art but in the necessity for poetic form, indeed, for anything aesthetic. As Auden puts it, again in "Spain 1937":

Tomorrow, for the young, the poets exploding like bombs,
The walks by the lake, the winter of perfect communion;
      Tomorrow the bicycle races
Through the suburbs on summer evenings; but today the
    struggle.

Today the inevitable increase in the chances of death;
The conscious acceptance of guilt in the fact of murder;
      Today the expending of powers
On the flat ephemeral pamphlet and the boring meeting.

Today the makeshift consolations; the shared cigarette;
The cards in the candle-lit barn and the scraping concert,
      The masculine jokes; today the
Fumbled and unsatisfactory embrace before hurting.

We do not, of course, find many passages like this in American poetry; but in the relatively few cases when American poets have renounced the inner life for immersion in "the struggle," we find the same pained astonishment at the drudgery of revolution and a paralyzing self-doubt at the writer's imminent loss of his or her own art. For example, in Adrienne Rich's "Leaflets," the speaker, marveling at her own suffering—"*that I can live half a year / as I have never lived up to this time*"—compares herself to "Chekhov coughing up blood almost daily," and later, invoking "the photograph / of dead Jewish terrorists, aged 15 / their faces wide-eyed," cries out: "What are we coming to / what wants these things of us / who wants them." In the last section of that poem, addressing a revolutionary compatriot, Rich tries, with a terrible humility, to plead the relevance of her poem to the struggle, to establish even the most tenuous grounds for her poem's use:

      I want to hand you this
leaflet streaming with rain or tears
      but the words coming clear
something you might find crushed into your hand
      after passing a barricade
and stuff in your raincoat pocket.
      I want this to reach you
who once told me that poetry is nothing sacred
      —no more sacred that is
than other things in your life—
      to answer yes, if life is uncorrupted
no better poetry is wanted.
      I want this to be yours

in the sense that if you find and read it
        it will be there in you already
and the leaflet then merely something
        to leave behind, a little leaf
in the drawer of a sublet room.

In this passage, just as in Forché's essay and in her poem to Des Pres, we see the poet's moving yet naive determination to deny the distinction between art and politics, between art and life itself. But the resulting utterance, although it has the ring of authentic anguish, authentic "engagement," is not especially good art. Under the stress of total political engagement, a person's art is apt to break down. Forché herself admits as much in "Return," a poem which documents her paranoia, culture shock, and moral bewilderment at the callous opulence of America compared to the nightmare of El Salvador, when she declares that "all manner of speaking / has failed":

        Josephine, I tell you
I have not slept, not since I drove
those streets with a gun in my lap,
not since all manner of speaking
has failed & the remnant of my life
continues onward. I go mad, for example,
in the Safeway, and the many heads
of lettuce, papayas & sugar, pineapples
& coffee, especially the coffee.

Like the other examples above, this passage is so overwhelmed by a sense of hysterical immediacy that it tempts one to look hard not only at Forché's ambiguous assertion that "what matters" in a poem is "the quality of its engagement," but also at some of the assumptions that underlie it, particularly her theory of composition.

*   *   *   *

Forché's claim that "what matters is not whether a poem is political, but the quality of its engagement" blurs a distinction which is, in fact, useful, by refusing to differentiate between political and nonpolitical human behavior. Her argument is a familiar one, of course, and it has a grain of truth to it. Every decision which we make, our choices in food, clothing, and recreation, *could* be construed as implicitly "political" in meaning. But the "meaning" of human actions, when it is derived in this manner, has a rather arbitrary and adventitious quality. Virtually *any* act could be seen as having political significance, if construed as implying all the possible political actions which the actor could have taken but did not. To buy a steak dinner (instead of eating more cheaply and devoting the savings in money to the cause of the oppressed) could be construed, from a radical perspective, as a de facto form of oppression. When viewed ideologically, a person's reasons for doing *anything* instead of something else can be judged. In much the same way that deconstructionist approaches to language make a mockery of the interpretation of texts, so do conventional radical denials of the distinction between "political" and "nonpolitical" behavior make a mockery of any attempt to interpret human behavior. It is one thing to purposefully support a candidate for political office. It is another thing to eat a steak. Even to suggest that these two human actions might have equal political and ideological significance is to lie. To claim, as Forché does, that "there is no such thing as a non-political poetry" is to redouble that lie while shrouding it within a second lie, namely the false notion that there is no distinction between "art" and "life." There *is* a distinction, one nowhere better made than by Barbara Herrnstein Smith when, in *Poetic Closure*, she reminds us of the difference between our responses to a death in a stage play and to the actual death of a friend or a relative.

"What matters," Forché writes, "is not whether a poem is political, but the quality of its engagement." If we assume for a moment that by "engagement" Forché means engagement in a political sense—engagement with history—then, it seems to me, we can rather easily find poems which, although written by authors whose "quality of engagement" with history is quite high, are poor, are nothing more than, as Forché herself puts it, "propagandistic hack-work." A good example of such a poem would be Allen Ginsberg's "Capitol Airlines," a monotonous succession of twenty-four quatrains listing things which "I don't like." Below are the first, the third, and the last:

> I don't like the government where I live
> I don't like dictatorship of the Rich

I don't like bureaucrats telling me what to eat
I don't like Police dogs sniffing round my feet
. . . .
I don't like Capitalists selling me gasoline Coke
Multinationals burning Amazon trees to smoke
Big Corporation takeover media mind
I don't like the Top-bananas that're robbing Guatemala blind
. . . .
Aware Aware wherever you are No Fear
Trust your heart Don't ride your Paranoia dear
Breathe together with an ordinary mind
Armed with Humor Feed & Help Enlighten Woe Mankind.

This is bad poetry. Because the poem discovers nothing, we discover nothing as we read it; nor are we drawn—as we would be by well-made art—to return to this poem. It is expendable. Yet the author has, as that sanctimonious expression runs, "paid his dues."

Conversely, we find, in the poetry of Wallace Stevens, work of the highest quality by an author whose "quality of engagement" with history, measured by the standards of Forché or any other committed poet, is abysmal. Indeed, Stevens can be, at times, overtly offensive even while producing good poetry. Consider, for example, these lines from "The News and the Weather," lines in which Stevens is trying to evoke the smell of a magnolia tree:

Solange, the magnolia to whom I spoke,
A nigger tree and with a nigger name,

To which I spoke, near which I stood and spoke,
I am Solange, euphonious bane, she said.

I am a poison at the winter's end,
Taken with withered weather, crumpled clouds,

To smother the wry spirit's misery.
Inhale the purple fragrance. It becomes

Almost a nigger fragment, a *mystique*
For the spirit left helpless by the intelligence.

There's a moment in the year, Solange,
When the deep breath fetches another year of life.

The lines use "nigger" in a consistently derogatory way, and the second line invokes a racial stereotype. Despite its racism, however, the poetry is good; the invention of the name "Solange"—the corny, pseudoexotic name of a heroine in a grade-D melodrama—along with the overlush "euphonious bane" as the "name" of the smell of a magnolia *is* brilliant and memorable, as is the overall portrayal of spring fragrance and spring fever as a cheap yet irresistible melodrama to which one wryly succumbs—Stevens's gloss, perhaps, on the notion of April as the "cruellest month."

Suppose, however, that by "quality of engagement" Forché means not the quality of one's actual engagement with history, but rather the quality of one's imagined engagement with the world and with language as one is, in her words, "taking pen to paper"—the quality of one's vision as it is clarified and shaped through the act of writing. Then the term "quality of engagement" *would* explain the discrepancy in quality between the Ginsberg sloganeering and Stevens's reactionary beauty. But this construction of the term would stand in direct contradiction to what Forché then insists upon when she declares that "the time . . . to determine what those politics will be is not the moment of taking pen to paper, but during the whole of one's life. We are responsible for the quality of our vision."

This contradiction in Forché's stance is one which any serious writer can appreciate. What she *wants* to argue, what she as a person committed to a political/moral ideology feels she *ought* to prove—that art which does not embody her ideology to the letter is worthless—contradicts what she, a brilliant writer herself, knows is true: that through the very act of writing we discover and clarify our vision, that particularly in a poem quality of vision depends, in large part, on the degree to which that poem discovers its vision through its composition, not on the quality of the author's previous political engagement.

All Forché's attempts in her essay to circumvent this contradiction fail. Just how shrewdly she tries to dodge it may be seen in her refusal to recognize the same contradiction in an argument by Hans Magnus Enzensburger, which she invokes in support of her position. "Enzensburger," she says, "has argued the futility of locating the political aspect of poetry outside poetry itself." She then quotes from Enzensburger:

. . . the bourgeois esthetic . . . would like to deny poetry any social aspect. Too often the champions of inwardness and sensibility are

reactionaries. They consider politics a special subject best left to pro-
fessionals. . . . For a political quarantine placed on poetry in the
name of eternal values, itself serves political ends.

She concludes: "Enzensburger is correct in stating 'The poem
expresses in exemplary fashion that it is not at the disposal of
politics. That is its political content.'"

Never mind that Forché has, a moment earlier, stated that
"there is no such thing as non-political poetry." Enzensburger's argument, as Forché paraphrases it, is the purest casuis-
try. He is arguing, in effect, that a poetry which is overtly
political and of a leftist persuasion, because it does not take
for granted the given political milieu, because it is "not at the
disposal of politics" (West Germany's bourgeois status quo), is
above politics, that the *most* political poetry is actually the
least political. In this argument, too, we find the distinction
between what is "political" and what is not "political" not
only confused: it is deliberately *reversed*. Just how extreme the
distortion is, how flagrantly it violates common sense and
makes a mockery of all distinctions, may be seen if we observe that even *within* the so-called "bourgeois esthetic" we
can distinguish between the political and the nonpolitical. For
example, Kipling's "The White Man's Burden" is more political
in content than Housman's "Loveliest of trees . . ."; similarly,
on the left, Neruda's love poems are less political than his invective against the United Fruit Company.

*   *   *   *

What, then, constitutes a "political" poem? If we discount
satire, we can define a political poem as follows: it is a poem
which overtly attempts to reveal connections between the
feelings—the inner life—of the individual, and objective economic and historical facts. To accept such a definition is to
assume, of course, that we can distinguish between what is
political and what is not; and that we can therefore distinguish between "political" and "artistic" engagement. If we
can, it then follows that good nonpolitical poems like the Stevens poem can come from low-quality political engagement
but high-quality artistic engagement, that poor political poems
like Ginsberg's "Capitol Airlines" can be the result of high-

quality political engagement but low-quality artistic engagement, and that there must also be a middle ground—a poem overtly political and evincing a sufficient quality of artistic *and* political engagement. To define this middle ground and evaluate its poetry, let us examine a truly excellent political poem, Louis Simpson's "On the Lawn at the Villa":

> On the lawn at the villa—
> That's the way to start, eh, reader?
> We know where we stand—somewhere expensive—
> You and I *imperturbes,* as Walt would say,
> Before the diversions of wealth, you and I *engagés.*
>
> On the lawn at the villa
> Sat a manufacturer of explosives,
> His wife from Paris,
> And a young man named Bruno,
>
> And myself, being American,
> Willing to talk to these malefactors,
> The manufacturer of explosives, and so on,
> But somehow superior. By that I mean democratic.
> It's complicated, being an American,
> Having the money and the bad conscience, both at the same
>   time.
> Perhaps, after all, this is not the right subject for a poem.
>
> We were all sitting there paralyzed
> In the hot Tuscan afternoon,
> And the bodies of the machine-gun crew were draped over
>   the balcony.
> So we sat there all afternoon.

Disregarding questions of poetic form, for the moment, and addressing only questions of rhetoric, why is the Simpson poem so much better not only than the Ginsberg, but better than Forché's "Return," Auden's "Spain 1937," or Rich's "Leaflets"?

"Capitol Airlines" offers its platitudes too smugly. Although I happen to agree with all of them, they lack moral authority. Nowhere do I feel that the speaker has questioned the assumptions behind his dogma. His propositions are as complacent and righteous as Reagan's clichés about the glories of "free enterprise." The poem's political opinions—its interpretation of political events—precede, indeed, have been thoroughly formulated long before, to borrow Forché's expression, "the moment of taking pen to paper." The poem's rhetoric consists of exactly what Ginsberg himself would call "media mind." As a result, it is unpersuasive.

For a similar reason, the note of hysteria and shock in both Forché poems, as in the Auden and Rich poems, seriously undermines their authority by bringing into question the speaker's judgment. Anger, fear, guilt, outrage: these emotions are so apt to distort the perceptions of an individual that when we encounter them in a poem, particularly when that poem questions its own raison d'être, as all these poems do, we lose confidence in the speaker, we recoil. Although the speaker's feelings in all of these poems are heartrendingly authentic, sincerity is not enough. Just as in "Capitol Airlines" the author's analysis of events was complete and fixed before he set pen to paper, in these poems the author's emotional disposition was overdetermined prior to "the moment of taking pen to paper." "Capitol Airlines" blurts ideology, "Return" blurts indignation. Both poems are written from the perspective of high-quality—i.e., deep and firsthand—political engagement; but it is the very "passionate intensity" of that engagement which corrupts their authors' artistic engagement.

The Simpson poem, on the other hand, like virtually all of the best political poetry in our century—for example, the poems of Brecht—is neither smug nor hysterical. Instead, it is analytic. The speaker's judgment is impaired neither by ideology nor excessive emotion. Faced with a situation which is "complicated," the poet, as he takes "pen to paper," has not totally made up his mind about anything. On the one hand, although the speaker feels "somehow superior" to the "malefactors," he is aware that his willingness to talk to them is a de facto form of complicity with a system of oppression which serves him, protects him even while he has a "bad conscience" about it. On the other hand, despite his moral discomfort among "malefactors," he is too worldly to cry, as Forché does toward the end of "Return," "We no longer resemble decent / men." Instead, he is "willing to talk" with them, willing to see them as human, willing to admit, empathetically, that the "hot Tuscan afternoon" sun democratizes all men with drowsiness, even the machine-gunners protecting the diversions of wealth which he enjoys here as well as at home, in America, among the upper-middle class. Every character in the Simpson tableau is granted human *feelings*.

In the word "paralyzed" all the poem's threads are drawn together. Everybody on the lawn—the speaker, the malefactors, the machine-gun crew—is "paralyzed" is his respective position in the scene as in the social system which created and which sustains the villa—paralyzed by his humanness, by a moral torpor grounded just as deeply in his nature as the torpor to which all humans, stretched out in the "hot Tuscan afternoon," succumb. Indeed, the poem presents physical and moral torpor as identical, mutually explanatory. Although Simpson's judgment is stern, it is realistic and ruthlessly honest; at the same time, it is too sophisticated to allow for hysteria, bitterness, or smugness.

Simpson's poem is, however, "analytic" in a far deeper sense than by virtue of its levelheadedness. We feel that the very poem is a *method* of analysis rather than the *product* of analysis, that the poem came into existence not as a vehicle for communicating some already discovered political vision but rather as a means by which, through the act of writing, the speaker might discover and clarify the precise connections between his feelings and troublesome political/economic facts: "It's complicated being an American." This sense of the final form of the poem as having been "discovered" rather than preordained is reinforced by the speaker's ironic nudges to the reader, "That's the way to start, eh, reader?" and the fifth line from the end: "Perhaps, after all, this is not the right subject for a poem." These nudges, which are integral to the poem's very form, are far different from Rich's disavowal of her poem as art, or Forchés declaration that "all manner of speaking / has failed." Simpson's nudges have more the sense: *You would like me to drop this sensitive subject—a subject which is liable to embarrass us all—by offering the excuse that it is not suitable for poetry. But I am going to pursue it until I myself fully understand and have found the right words for this intimation which I wish to clarify.* Simpson's ultimate clarification of his "complicated" situation is arrived at with the word "paralyzed."

*   *   *   *

The reasons for the quality of the Simpson poem are, as they have to be, the same reasons which determine when any poem, political or not, is good. It exhibits a close relation between "form" and "content," a relation whose closeness, as Charles O. Hartman has pointed out and as has come to be widely understood, is best regarded not so much as the end product of some premeditated strategy but as evidence of events which took place during the process of composition. The degree to which the Simpson poem works is the degree to which the poet, in attempting to clarify an obscure but nagging set of connections, *discovered* the poem's final version, and, in discovering that—how to say something—discovered what it was he had wanted to say. All other factors being equal, then, the better a poem the more fully *realized* it will be, its degree of realization varying in direct proportion to the degree to which evidence of the poem's discovery of its form—be it through rhetoric, prosody, or structure—may be discerned in that final version. It is this "evidence" which, on reading after reading, will lend the best poem its tantalizing strangeness yet rightness, what William Stafford has called "the live form." In the Simpson poem it is present not only in the odd asides to the reader but in the poem's overall sense of struggle. At every point in the text we feel the author moving blocks of material around, weighing them, letting them settle, and stepping back to check their placement. We have a pronounced sense of all the uneasy trial and error lying behind the speaker's final choice of diction, for example the uneasy diction of "Willing to talk to these malefactors" instead of, say, "Content to get along with these profiteers" or "Not ashamed to chat with these villains" or the innumerable other possibilities.

For similar reasons, perhaps the best political poem, as I have defined "political" poetry, in *The Country Between Us* is Forché's prose poem "The Colonel":

What you have heard is true. I was in his house. His wife carried a tray of coffee and sugar. His daughter filed her nails, his son went out for the night. There were daily papers, pet dogs, a pistol on the cushion beside him. The moon swung bare on its black cord over the house. On the television was a cop show. It was in English. Broken bottles were imbedded in the walls around the house to scoop the kneecaps from a man's legs or cut his hands to lace. On the windows there were gratings as there are in liquor stores. We had dinner, rack of lamb, good wine, a gold bell on the table for calling the maid. The maid brought green mangoes, salt, a type of bread. I was asked how I enjoyed the country. There was a brief commercial in Spanish. His wife took everything away. There was some talk then of how difficult it had become to govern. The parrot said hello on the terrace. The colonel told it to shut up, and pushed himself from the table. My friend said to me with his eyes: say nothing. The colonel returned with a sack as is used to bring groceries home. He spilled many human ears on the table. They were like dried peach halves. There is no other way to say this. He took one of them in his hands, shook it in our faces, dropped it into a water glass. It came alive there. I am tired of fooling around, he said. As for the rights of anyone, tell your people they can go fuck themselves. He swept the ears to the floor with his arm and raised the last of his wine in the air. Something for your poetry, no? he said. Some of the ears on the floor caught this scrap of his voice. Some of the ears on the floor were pressed to the ground.

Why is this poem so good? Because the speaker/author's ideological predispositions do not preempt authentic poetic discovery—the discovery of connections between the feel of her individual life and, in this case, objective, historical and economic facts, discovery which is directly carried over into the poem's language and structure, a structure which, by matter-of-factly in a catalogue format juxtaposing such items as "daily papers, pet dogs, a pistol on the cushion . . . gratings as there are in liquor stores," not only links oppression inevitably with bourgeois life but also reveals the profound banality of such evil, a banality epitomized finally by the ears "like dried peach halves" in what might be the Salvadoran equivalent to a brown paper Safeway shopping bag. The poem is "analytic" in precisely the sense that the Simpson poem is. Instead of delivering us a conclusion, it renders the process of analysis itself. Indeed, Forché herself seems to sense how much it is authorial discovery *after* "pen" has been taken to "paper" which lends this poem its power. Introducing it, she characterizes it as "almost a *poème trouvé*." Of course, "The Colonel" is nothing like a "found" poem. The "found" poem simply rearranges some nonpoetic discourse as verse, whereas this poem not only lacks verse, but it is in Forché's own words. It is *"trouvé"* in a more profound sense, in the sense that all excellent poetry is. In its genuine wonderment and curiosity at the details of the colonel's household, at the way in which bourgeois banalities are stored so casually side by side with the trappings of oppression (as if those furnishings naturally belonged together), it discovers and renders these connections more forcibly than any ideological statement could.

*   *   *   *

If, as I have tried to suggest and as the examples above seek to demonstrate, a necessary (though not sufficient) condition for any poem to succeed is that it discover its intentions through its very composition, then we can begin to appreciate why it is rather more difficult to write good poems on political themes than on other themes; for in the domain of politics our minds and our emotions are more often than not made up, just as Forché mistakenly says they should be, before we take pen to paper. Of course, it would be simplistic to conclude that all poems are either overdetermined or else wholly successful "discoveries." More often, we find in poems degrees of "discovery." As an example of two poems, each with some (but a different degree of) merit, and of the relation between "discovery" and merit, let us compare the following two poems about prisoners. The first is by Charles Simic:

> The Prisoner
>
> He is thinking of us.
> These leaves, their lazy rustle
> That made us sleepy after lunch
> So we had to lie down.
>
> He considers my hand on her breast,
> Her closed eyelids, her moist lips
> Against my forehead, and the shadows of trees
> Hovering on the ceiling.
>
> It's been so long. He has trouble
> Deciding what else is there.
> And all along the suspicion
> That we do not exist.

The Simic poem is the brilliant solution to a problem: how to clarify the obscurely sensed connections between the routinely pleasurable feel of your life and your knowledge that, at this very moment, there exist prisoners whose suffering you would just as soon put out of mind. What I have termed "evidence" of discovery may be appreciated if we imagine Simic trying to start the poem not with "He is thinking of us. / These leaves . . ." but with "We are thinking of *him* / Those rats . . ." and ending not with "And all along the suspicion / That we do not exist" but rather with "And all along our suspicion / That he does not exist." The failure of such a poem would have been a foregone conclusion. The text would have had to consist of an obligatory catalogue of horrors: the smell of excrement, rats, the brutality of guards, bad food, darkness, boredom, and so on. The poem's main discovery is structural, a startling reversal of perspective, a reversal by which Simic not only maximizes the discrepancy between the conditions of the prisoner and the speaker but also suggests the symbiotic relationship between them. The speaker recognizes the injustice of his pleasure—of all pleasure—but would certainly not trade places with the prisoner. If anything, the speaker's contented realization that he is not in the prisoner's shoes sharpens his capacity to savor the moment. The poem operates insidiously. The pleasures of life as a winner—as a de facto oppressor—are too great to turn down, though their very availability may be directly dependent on somebody's misery.

How essential structural "discovery" is to the Simic poem may be appreciated if we compare that poem with the following piece by Forché—a poem which, though quite strong, is not as fully realized as "The Prisoner."

The Visitor

In Spanish he whispers there is no time left.
It is the sound of scythes arching in wheat,
the ache of some field song in Salvador.
The wind along the prison, cautious
as Francisco's hands on the inside, touching
the walls as he walks, it is his wife's breath
slipping into his cell each night while he
imagines his hand to be hers, it is a small country.
There is nothing one man will not do to another.

What is missing here? First, the relation between the speaker and the prisoner, instead of being explored, is taken for granted. Second, the ending of the Forché poem has only the ring of a truism. By announcing the last line as if it were fresh information, the speaker loses some moral authority.

Because the Forché poem does not, then, discover its angle of vision in process, it remains only very skillful propaganda, the communication of an already held opinion, an example of how when artistic and political engagement become confused, that lack of "conviction" so necessary a precondition for a good poem may, in the best cause, be corrupted by that very "passionate intensity" which is a necessary ingredient of high-quality *political* engagement such as Forché's. The limits of what Forché calls a "poetry of witness," like the already well-documented limits of a poetry of confession, lie in the temptations to excess, in a poetic which all too quickly can become only an iterated, mechanical cry of pain, making an ideology of guilt and outrage, a rhetoric without the authority of discovered vision.

6. "Discovered Form" and the Structure of Intention

In his brilliant book-length essay on prosody, *Free Verse* (Princeton University Press, 1980), a book which uses the topic of prosody as an approach to questions about "poetic form," Charles O. Hartman coins the evocative term "discovered form" to describe "not a form, but a way of thinking about poetic forms. It presents form not as a product but a process, not as structure but as operation." Hartman's paradigm of a poem that "discovers" its "form" is Wallace Stevens's "Valley Candle":

> My candle burned alone in an immense valley.
> Beams of the huge night converged upon it,
> Until the wind blew.
> Then beams of the huge night
> Converged upon its image
> Until the wind blew.

Of this poem, Hartman writes:

Reading "Valley Candle," we do not deduce a theme and then appreciate how deftly Stevens uses form. We examine the form and from it abstract a theme: that when internal and external experience have identical structures, subjects and objects become interchangeable. . . . The poem represents two events in identical language because they are identical in structure. Thus the linguistic repetition precisely reflects the theme. . . . In short, form and content are inseparable. This is a commonplace; the poem exhibits "unity," meshing its formal and material causes.

Hartman's demonstration is a little confusing here, because of minor sloppiness. He uses the terms "form" and "structure" more or less interchangeably; and, because of the vagueness of the term "form," he perhaps overstates the poem's "unity." For example, the prosody of the Stevens poem is, presumably, an element of its "form." Yet we could certainly change the lineation of the poem without disturbing the syntactical arrangement that is responsible for the "unity" which Hartman adduces.

In the next paragraph, however, Hartman makes the leap crucial to his formulation:

Yet the formal cause is equally linked with an efficient cause, the maker—or rather the making of the poem. Meaning arises not from what the poem says, but from what it does and the doing that it represents. It cannot be reduced to either a content (a set of propositions) or a form, in the sense in which that word complements "content"—an achieved product, a static structure. Nor, indeed, can meaning be reduced to an accomplished combination or unity of form and content. We comprehend the poem only as a process, not as an object. . . . "My candle" . . . is no single abstracted faculty of the human mind, but the speaker himself in his act of speaking. . . . The form of "Valley Candle" encourages us to identify with the implied author's experience by reducing our separation from him, since the form is as new to him as it is to us. . . . "Discovery" seems the best name for this whole experience or process or rhetorical method.

One feels intuitively that Hartman's instructions about how to read "Valley Candle" (as well as many other contemporary poems) are correct, even though his formulation continues to exhibit minor confusions, confusions which arise, as much as anything, from Hartman's deployment of the word "form"—a word with such an endless range of reference that, because Hartman refuses to define it beyond letting it be roughly synonymous with "structure" (whose meaning he also assumes), it becomes, in context, virtually meaningless. We notice, for example, that in the passage above he simply contradicts his earlier assertion that there is a "unity" between the poem's "form" and "content." We notice also that in his attempt to stress the dynamic aspect of "this particular poem's content—'meaning' as a participle, not a noun"—he somewhat overstates his case: "We comprehend the poem *only* [my italics] as a process." He refuses categorically to admit that "My candle" might carry any symbolic meaning. Indeed, we begin to sense that perhaps "Valley Candle" is not the most ideal example which Hartman could have found to illustrate "discovery" of "form." The poem is a little too tidy; both its parallel syntactical blocks nest together like bricks in one-to-one correspondence. The poem's binary structure is far more static than if the poem had consisted of *three* or more units which, because no immediate meaning could have been imputed to the relation between them, would have more clearly illustrated process—the movement of the implied author's mind from one possibility to the next, and so on. Even a three-unit sonata structure would have exhibited more of a sense of movement: a dialectical process of (1) thesis; (2) antithesis; (3) synthesis. Surely a longer, more discursive, conversational poem might have served as a more apt example of "meaning as a participle"—a poem such as *Song of Myself*, which does seem to dramatize the process of "discovery" of its "form" as it goes along.

Nevertheless, despite the rough edges of Hartman's presentation, his concept of "discovered form" represents, I believe, the best extant critical description we have of an important new way of reading much of our contemporary poetry—particularly the lyric and the short "meditative" or narrative conversation poem—a way of reading which, though it need not and should not replace standard New-Critical approaches to interpretation, constitutes a necessary supplement to them. All that Hartman's formulation needs are a few refinements, refinements which I will now propose.

* * * *

The ambiguities in Hartman's formulation of "discovered form" are, I think, the result of three related problems: (1) he never adequately defines the terms "form" and "structure"; (2) although he is clearly aware that the implications of "discovered form" challenge that rankling critical blue law known as "the Intentional Fallacy," he remains too respectful of it; (3) by relying as heavily as he does upon "Valley Candle," a poem whose implied author remains relatively hidden and whose structure is relatively static, he deprives himself of possibly more persuasive demonstrations.

The source of Hartman's imprecision lies in the first of these problems, in the limitations of his terminology—a terminology which literally forces him, at times, into corners, leading him to contradict himself. In every instance where Hartman uses the term "form," the term "thematic structure," as developed by Barbara Herrnstein Smith in *Poetic Closure*, would have been more descriptive; for unless the term "form" is used to refer to some category—to a so-called "fixed form" such as the heroic couplet or the sonnet—it is so open-ended as to be virtually meaningless. Indeed, it is for just this reason that, in her development of a working definition for "poetic structure," Smith restricts the term "form" to refer to elements of prosody:

The division of structural principles into two kinds, formal and thematic, corresponds to a more general division which, because it is inherent in the double nature of language, can be observed in all the elements of a poem. *Formal elements* are defined as those which arise from the physical nature of words, and would include such features as rhyme, alliteration, and syllabic meter. The *thematic elements* of a poem are those which arise from the symbolic or conventional nature of words, and to which only someone familiar with the language could respond; they would include everything from reference to syntax to tone.

What does Herrnstein Smith mean by "structure"?

It will be useful to regard the structure of a poem as consisting of the principles by which it is generated or according to which one element follows another. The description of a poem's structure, then, becomes the answer to the question, "What keeps it going?"

If the "formal structure" of a poem is its prosody, then the "formal structure" of a sonnet—what "keeps it going" for fourteen lines and rhyming in one pattern or another—is dictated by the prosodic rules that define the convention called "the sonnet." It is worth noting, however, that (1) such a prosody may or may not bear any relation to what the poem is about; (2) in free verse it is much more difficult than in a fixed-form poem to identify "the principles by which . . . one element follows another." Indeed, perhaps the only way is through trial and error, by substituting, for the original, different wordings with their accompanying sound, and then estimating the net gain or loss to the poem.

The "thematic structure" of a poem, or what I will, henceforth, call its "structure," is the way in which a poem's subject matter is developed. And we might note that just because we can refer to the "structure" of a poem does not mean that every poem exhibits it. To take a simple, famous example, let us try to ascertain the "structure" of Joyce Kilmer's "Trees":

I think that I shall never see
A poem lovely as a tree.

A tree whose hungry mouth is pressed
Against the earth's sweet flowing breast;

A tree that looks to God all day,
And lifts her leafy arms to pray;

A tree that may in summer wear
A nest of robins in her hair;

Upon whose bosom snow has lain;
Who intimately lives with rain.

Poems are made by fools like me,
But only God can make a tree.

It takes little imagination to see that if we remove some of the middle stanzas of this poem or alter their order, or both, the poem's net meaning remains virtually unchanged. The poem simply has *no* structure: there is no discernible reason why "one [thematic] element follows another," and certainly no satisfying answer to the question "What keeps it going?"

Smith's conception of structure, "What keeps it going," suggests another small difficulty in Hartman's approach to "Valley Candle." He overstates the case of "Valley Candle" as a poem of process, because he does not sufficiently acknowledge that poetic structure has a dual aspect: it is both static and dynamic. Northrop Frye expresses this duality very neatly in *The Great Code*:

Reading words in sequence . . . is the first of two critical operations. Once a verbal structure is read, and reread often enough to be possessed, it "freezes." It turns into a unity in which all parts exist at once, which we can then examine like a picture, without regard to the specific movement of the narrative. We may compare it to the study of a musical score, where we can turn to any part of it without regard to sequential performance. The term "structure," which we have used so often, is a metaphor from architecture, and may be misleading when we are speaking of narrative, which is not a simultaneous structure but a movement in time. The term "structure" comes into its proper context in the second stage, which is where discussion of "spatial form" and kindred critical topics take their origin.

Smith is very much aware of this same duality when she writes: "'What keeps it going?' To think of poetic structure this way, rather than as an organization of, or relationship among, elements, is to emphasize the temporal and dynamic qualities that poetry shares with music." If we construe the term "structure" as Frye and Smith do, it comprehends quite handily both the static and dynamic aspects of "Valley Candle." The "static" interpretation of the poem's structure could very well recapitulate Hartman's own words: "The poem represents two events in identical language because they are identical in structure." In order to interpret the "discovered" aspect of the poem's structure, however, we would seek a more precise formulation than Hartman provides. Inherent in the notion of "discovery" is the notion of a search, in short, of sequence: first this, then this, then this. Search leads to discovery. And inherent in the notion of sequence is the notion of an elapsed temporal interval.

> My candle burned alone in an immense valley.
> Beams of the huge night converged upon it,
> Until the wind blew.
> Then beams of the huge night
> Converged upon its image
> Until the wind blew.

Short as it is, "Valley Candle" is permeated with a sense of time, both in the tenses of its verbs and in its adverbs: "burned . . . Until . . . Then . . . Converged . . . Until." Viewed this way, the poem is an apt illustration of Smith's proposal that "the description of a poem's structure . . . becomes the answer to the question, 'What keeps it going'"; for, as Smith suggests, "it allows the possibility of a corollary question, namely, 'What stops it from going?'" The first half of the poem is answered by the second part, so that the poem appears to dramatize the very mental process—the very act of composition—whereby its final "structure" is "discovered." If we let ourselves enact, in our minds, the poem's structure as a *sequence*, we imagine it taking place over an interval of time during which the author set down the first two sentences and, from them, "discovered" the rest, the ending. In other words, inherent in the temporal, dynamic approach to poetic structure as a sequence is the possibility of the reader's vicarious participation in the very process of poetic composition as it originally took place over time, when the author was grappling with exactly those questions which Smith suggests define "poetic structure," namely the question "What keeps it going?" and the "corollary question . . . 'What stops it from going?'" Hartman himself very cautiously suggests as much when, speaking of "Valley Candle," he writes that in order to read it properly "we must search out the circumstances of the utterance. That is the context in which the poem will make sense. This search involves questions about the speaker—why he speaks, the situation in which he speaks, and so on." Hartman is even more explicit when he says that "discovered form" implies, like the notion of "organic" form, "not only 'unity' of form (in the sense of structure) with content," but "*a theory of the genesis of poems* [my italics]. Keats expressed this theory by demanding that poetry come to the poet 'as naturally as leaves to a tree.' But modern critics, particularly since Wimsatt and Beardsley published their attack on the 'Intentional Fallacy,' have avoided speculating about the origins of poems, and so tended to ignore this second implication."

There are two ways by which Hartman could have avoided coming to terms with the Intentional Fallacy. He chooses the safer of the two, and it is the wrong one. He reverts to a theory of mimesis:

The word ["discovered"] implies both invention and revelation. . . . At the moment, the point is that such a form represents an experience shared by the reader and the poet—or at least the poet's mimetic representative in the poem, the speaker. . . . The unique structure of "Valley Candle" lends poignancy and immediacy to our impression of discovery. For a poet seeking this effect, free verse seems a logical strategy. But it is not the only one.

Scrupulous as Hartman is here, in one crucial way his choice of diction falsifies both his own case and, perhaps, misrepresents the very nature of poetry: he implies that the reader's "impression of discovery" can derive merely from a calculated "effect" produced by a "logical strategy." The connotations of "impression," of "effect," of "logical," and of "strategy" not only contradict all the carefully assembled connotations of Hartman's own term, "discovery"; but Hartman's implication that "discovery" is achieved through calculation flies squarely in the face of what poets themselves, from Keats to Frost, have testified about the process of composition—that discovery is not the result of calculation but must, if a poem is to move the reader, come as an authentic surprise. As Frost put it in "The Figure a Poem Makes":

It is but a trick poem and no poem at all if the best of it was thought of first and saved for the last. It finds its own name as it goes and discovers the best waiting for it in some final phrase at once wise and sad . . . . No tears for the writer, no tears in the reader. Nor surprise for the writer, no surprise for the reader. For me the initial delight is in the surprise of remembering something I didn't know I knew. . . . It [a poem] must be a revelation, or a series of revelations, as much for the poet as for the reader. For it to be there must have been the greatest freedom of the material to move about in it and to establish relations in it regardless of time and space. . . . A poem may be worked over once it is in being, but may not be worried into being. Its most precious quality will remain its having run itself and carried away the poet with it. Read a hundred times, it will forever keep its freshness as a metal keeps its fragrance: it can never lose its sense of a meaning that once unfolded by surprise as it went.

*   *   *   *

Frost's description of poetic discovery is accurate. But if the concept of achieved poetic structure as something "discovered" is to be critically viable, there needs to be developed a practical strategy for talking about poetic structure in this manner. As Raymond Carney says of the editions of Wordsworth's poems being issued by Cornell University Press, which display in detail the various drafts of Wordsworth's major poems: "If we are to handle this material at all, we will need a *new* New Criticism, and will have to be prepared for a critical revolution more radical than anything since the upheavals of the old New Criticism thirty years ago." Indeed, New-Critical methodology, despite its positivist rigor, has implicitly and drastically misrepresented, in Carney's words, "what it is to author a text":

Texts were talked about as if they were simply willed into existence in a final draft form. Drafts previous to the final one were treated as if they were merely imperfect approximations of the later form or steps along the road toward its inevitable production. If manuscripts were consulted it was generally only to argue how the writer had progressively improved, clarified, or (sometimes) spoiled the Platonic form of his ideal well-made text.

As Carney points out, this ridiculous conception of a text arose from a temptation toward a methodological purity which ultimately had little concern for truth:

> . . . the entirely salutary assumption that all one's critical evidence must originate in the text (and not in biography, history, or personal statements) was transformed into the entirely unsalutary conclusion that all one's critical observations must terminate with it. Consequently, when conclusions about a writer's desires, intentions, and consciousness were not entirely eliminated from critical discourse, they were allowed to be invoked only in the most fugitive and unsystematic ways. One of the more comical results was that certain psychological statements were allowed into critical discourse as long as they were descriptions of the text under study and not of the mind or personality that produced it. A poem might have "tension" without the poet being said to be "tense" . . . .

Hartman is rather more polite than Carney. As he puts it, almost plaintively, "I do not mean to dispute the arguments against the Intentional Fallacy. And yet, as Wayne Booth has recognized by inventing the term 'implied author,' the reader cannot help but believe that the poem comes from somewhere." Hartman's notion of "discovered form," however, clearly suggests that if we are to adequately read a poem like "Valley Candle," we *must* commit the Intentional Fallacy, commit it not merely with impunity but even systematically. For, as Hartman suggests, the very subject matter of "Valley Candle" *is* the process of structural "discovery." To put it differently, "Valley Candle," like a great many of our best modernist and contemporary poems, is a dramatization of the process by which its author "discovered" his "intention." No wonder that when we read such a poem we derive, however indirectly or obscurely, some sense of a temporal sequence of mental events in the author leading up to this "discovery." Even if we cannot actually reconstruct the details of that sequence or empirically verify the order of events that made it up, we must, if we are to accurately interpret this type of poem, somehow admit into critical discussion this "sense" of the author's struggle *in the poem* to locate through experimentation the structure that will define his intention. It is this struggle, after all, that is, in large part, what the poem is really *about*.

*   *   *   *

The problems of talking about discovered intentionality, however, are formidable, perhaps insurmountable; for as Frost's description of composition—"No surprise for the writer, no surprise for the reader"—makes clear, inherent in the notion of discovered poetic structure is a value judgment. Discovered structure is a characteristic only of *achieved* poems, of poems which, in workshop parlance, "work." The very concept of discovered structure, then, assumes that we can generally agree at once on which poems are good and which are not; and that we can do this without applying a criterion of prior intentionality, without asking such naive questions as "What was the author's intention, and did the poem realize that intention?" Instead, the reader's apprehension of discovery will always begin as an intuitive value judgment: an initial, visceral response of pleasure, awe, a shock of recognition at the strangeness yet rightness of a given poem, followed by a gradual sense of intellectual pleasure as, through successive rereadings, he begins to get a sense of how the poem's structure works, as he duplicates, in effect, through a process which Marvin Bell has called "the technique of rereading," the process of discovery which the author underwent, until finally the reader begins to appreciate at an intellectual level the logic of the poem's unfolded structure. It is a logic—how one thing leads to the next—which the reader must piece together from what I can only think of as "evidence" which was "left behind" (as it were) in the text. What is the evidence *of*? As in action painting, it is evidence of the stress and drama and sequence of composition. What form does such evidence take? It may be prosodic. It may be rhetorical. It may, as in "Valley Candle," be the poem's structure itself. A good example of a relatively traditional-looking poem which nevertheless exhibits evidence of discovery is Frost's own "Spring Pools":

> These pools that, though in forests, still reflect
> The total sky almost without defect,

And like the flowers beside them, chill and shiver,
Will like the flowers beside them soon be gone,
And yet not out by any brook or river,
But up by roots to bring dark foliage on.

The trees that have it in their pent-up buds
To darken nature and be summer woods—
Let them think twice before they use their powers
To blot out and drink up and sweep away
These flowery waters and these watery flowers
From snow that melted only yesterday.

The poem marches on rather pleasantly and crisply, without astonishing us, until the epiphany of the penultimate line. Without the eleventh line, the poem would simply lack a raison d'être. We feel, immediately, as if the entire poem had been constructed for that line, a line which comes as a surprise and which, without the surrounding context, has a beauty that is so strange as to seem almost nonsensical. Indeed, the very strangeness of this line—its unforeseeable quality—is prime evidence of its "discovered" origin. It has the sense of a revelation. Obviously it is impossible to determine, without manuscript evidence, whether the eleventh line was the germinal line for the poem, whether the line occurred to Frost late in the composition of the poem or somewhere in the middle. But it does not matter. All that matters is that the relation between line eleven and its supporting context seems at once surprising yet inevitable. Perhaps the thoroughly pedestrian information preceding line eleven—that trees absorb water of melted snow in order to make leaves, that in this way the seasons are linked, and that this natural process is a rapid one—precipitated line eleven. Perhaps line eleven came first, and the rest of the poem was suggested by it. Both possibilities are equally plausible: (1) that line eleven reveals the "discovered" significance of otherwise pedestrian information; (2) that the rest of the poem begins to clarify the "discovered" significance—a raw, rather unsettling view of things—inherent in line eleven: a view which reveals that beneath the illusion of temporal sequence all things exist simultaneously in absolute contingency, flowery water with watery flower, a confusion of season and season, of vegetable and mineral, mind and matter, a contingency not merely imaged in the "pools" but nakedly revealed in the reflection of the flowers in the water, a reflection so revelatory that its shock is carried over into the language of line eleven, so that its very words reflect each other contingently, in a giddy moment of surrender to universal flux.

Regardless of which came prior to which, line eleven or its context, they illuminate one another in a logically consistent enough way that the poem exhibits what the New Critics called "tension," the very term which, as deployed in New Critical terminology, Carney justifiably ridicules. The poem's tension is structural, and it directs our attention back to the poem's composition. "Tension," in "Spring Pools," is evidence of "discovery." It points to the *author's* "tension"—his surprise at seeing an unsuspected set of connections—a surprise carried over into a set of discovered *linguistic* connections. Such a poem is an act of noticing so thoroughly realized in language that we might almost say that the act of noticing is made possible *by means of* language, here through a moment of vision that can be no less beautiful and unsettling than the words for it, the words *of* it. And we can begin to see why a standard New-Critical interpretation of "Spring Pools" is seriously incomplete. To be sure, the poem is about mutability, the interpenetration of the seasons, and the brevity of things. But it is also about its own act of discovery—about the author's revelation by means of language. The poem's story, then, is not only about what the author discovered one day in spring. It is also about discoveries which the poet made *in the poem*. In this respect, every poem exhibiting evidence of "discovery" will exhibit some degree—but only *some*—of self-reflexivity.

A more contemporary and equally beautiful poem conspicuously dramatizing the discovery of its own structure is Stanley Plumly's "Peppergrass":

> Nothing you could know, or name, or say
> in your sleep, nothing you'd remember,
> poor-man's-pepper, wildflower, weed—
> what the guidebook calls *the side*
> *of the road*—as from the moon the earth
> looks beautifully anonymous, this field
> pennycress, this shepherd's purse, nothing
> you could see: summer nights we'd look up
> at the absolute dark, the stars, and turn like toys. . .

Nothing you could hold on to
but the wet grass, cold as morning.

We were windmills where the wind came from,
nothing, nothing you could name,
blowing the lights out, one by one.

Like most of Plumly's best poems, this one is a poem of memory and is frankly nostalgic, recalling a rural and economically humble past when "we" in line eight were "nothing." Like "Valley Candle," "Peppergrass" cannot be adequately explicated in a traditional or New-Critical manner alone; for much of its content inheres in the dynamics of its structure, in the way in which one thing leads to the next. The poem begins by proposing a metaphor: "We" (the poem's subject, eventually denoted in line eight) were once as "anonymous" and beneath notice as roadside vegetation, as the earth itself when viewed from a sufficient distance. Implicit in this metaphor is, of course, the attitude which the poem gradually discovers: that the plants on the roadside, the ignored of the world, though they are invisible as any individual human being on the earth if viewed from the moon, are just as sensitive and hold their experience just as sacred as the passing observer, who is the reader himself passing through *Out-of-the-Body Travel*, looking in at an entire world which, if only casually skimmed over, would remain merely "beautifully anonymous."

But the poem's power derives less from its metaphoric structure than from the way in which one thing follows another. We do not need to know that, as Plumly has testified, this poem was composed almost pell-mell at a single sitting, in order to *feel* the poem's unfolding sense of discovery. Evidence of such "discovery" abounds both in the poem's voice and in its pace. The poem hurries ahead in its quiet, earnest, almost apologetic tone, without irony, reciting the ways in which "we" were "nothing." Discovery is evidenced also in syntax, in the absence of a singular, first-person pronoun. Indeed, so humble is the speaker's posture before remembered experience that it is as if the poem forgets that there is any protagonist at all, before "we" is mentioned almost as an afterthought. The egolessness of the poem's syntax is further evidenced in its lack of verbs: the poem contains only two short independent clauses, virtually buried (like small, hidden selves in the weeds) within a lovingly recited list of nouns, all linked with the faithfully alleged "nothing . . . nothing." One imagines the poet, half-entranced, whispering these words to himself, treasuring each one like an amulet, trying to breathe it to life. In the beginning, the nouns are generic—wildflower, weed—but they become increasingly particular—moon, earth, pennycress. Then, at once, the reader and the author discover what these words had been all along: they are *names*. The names of what? The names of all that had been without a name—had been literally "anonymous"—the names of experience itself, experience so common—the stars on summer nights, the wet grass on summer mornings, roadside grass milling in the wind—that we had ceased to notice it. A poem which had started out as a list of nouns and turned into a list of names has become, with line nine, a list of images; and the pace of recitation slows, lengthening out along line nine as if to savor it, then comes to an almost complete stop to linger over the tantalizing wet-grass image, set apart in its own stanza. Finally, with a slight puff of "wind," the pace picks up again, as if the poem's last names were already being whirled away by time; and we understand, at last, what this poem is. It is a dramatization of the poet's discovery of how the very act of naming redeems experience, can rescue even the humblest aspects of experience from "anonymity" and restore the sacredness of life itself. We have been watching a process in which words, passionately meant, turn into names before our very eyes, so that "nothing" becomes synonymous with its antonym. And we realize that this is really what the poem is about: its own capability—about the dawning intention of its own redemptive process as it utters itself.

In the Frost poem the most pronounced evidence of discovery is rhetorical, in the context of the eleventh line, and structural, in the relation of line eleven to the remainder of the poem. In the Plumly poem, we find evidence of structural discovery at a deeper level, a level as fundamental as in "Valley Candle." The deeper the level of structural discovery, the more self-reflexive a poem tends to be. Evidence of discovery can also be prosodic. A good example of a poem displaying rather conspicuous evidence of prosodic discovery would be one I have previously mentioned in Chapter 1: Gary Gildner's "First Practice," in which the speaker, presumably an adult and, by Gildner's own testimony, the poet himself, is recalling his first football practice in eighth grade. The poem reads:

> After the doctor checked to see
> we weren't ruptured,
> the man with the short cigar took us
> under the grade school,
> where we went in case of attack
> or storm, and said
> he was Clifford Hill, he was
> a man who believed dogs
> ate dogs, he had once killed
> for his country, and if
> there were any girls present
> for them to leave now.
>   No one
> left. OK, he said, he said I take
> that to mean you are hungry
> men who hate to lose as much
> as I do. OK. Then
> he made two lines of us
> facing each other,
> and across the way, he said,
> is the man you hate most
> in the world,
> and if we are to win
> that title I want to see how.
> But I don't want to see
> any marks when you're dressed,
> he said. He said, *Now*.

In this poem, particularly in the first half, the speaker's attitude is dramatized by line breaks quite as much as by diction. Each line break creates a suspense which is immediately, as we turn the corner to the line below, deflated by a revelation which is pointedly banal: "took us / under the grade school"; "he was / a man"; "he had once killed / for his country." These line breaks dramatize the dual attitude of the speaker, who, while he remembers how melodramatic the football rite of passage had seemed at the time, can now, from his adult perspective, appreciate its essential emptiness and banality. He can perceive the mechanical, demythologized quality of the ritual—a ritual designed to awe boys but whose terms consisted of clichés. The line breaks, then, embody simultaneously both perspectives: traumatic excitement undercut by a slightly cynical detachment.

The "discovery" which we find in "First Practice" is not merely prosodic, however. Deflation of melodramatic memory is discovered rhetorically as well as prosodically: it is partly the product of beautifully timed clichéd diction. In fact, if we examine any achieved poem, we find that the three types of discovery which I have categorized as "rhetorical," "prosodic," and "structural" are all deeply implicated. In "Spring Pools," for example, the rhetorical strangeness of line eleven generated the structural tension redeeming the rest of the poem. In the Plumly poem, rhetorical discovery, a modulation from generic terms to names to images, lent the poem's list structure its dramatic impact. We might wonder, however, whether certain types of evidence of discovery are not more likely to show up in conjunction with certain poetic modes and conventions.

Hartman suggests that "prosodic discovery" is more pronounced in free verse:

Still, the principle of discovered form has a special bearing on nonmetrical prosody. Its most far-reaching effect is to create the possibility . . . of a prosody that will shift in its details from one line to the next, as the poem demands. . . . discovery can be seen as requiring a new prosodic flexibility. . . . When rhythm renounces the support of abstract or independent systems . . . the basic principle of the line emerges and takes absolute control. . . . The details of its rhythm are discovered (by poet and reader) with what it says; they are "organically" united.

My inclination is to doubt Hartman's supposition here. First, his suggestion that in free verse (any "non-numerical prosody") rhythm necessarily "renounces the support of abstract or independent systems" is simply wrong. If we look at "First Practice," for example, we see that within most of the syntactic units, i.e., between natural pauses, there are three stresses, and that the poem establishes this trimeter "norm" right at its outset: "AF-ter the DOCtor CHECKED (pause) to SEE / we WEREN'T RUPtured, / (pause) the MAN with the SHORT ciGAR (pause) TOOK us / UNder the GRADE school, (pause)," and so on. The poem's rhythm is not strictly held to this "norm," but the norm is conspicuous enough that its effect, augmented by a fairly high number of dactyls and anapests, makes the reader pleasantly conscious that the poem's speech is more highly organized than ordinary speech. By this means, "First Practice" manages to negotiate the difficult and paradoxical demands of resembling normal conversation yet being obviously art-speech as well.

Similarly, Plumly's "Peppergrass" exhibits a prosodic norm corresponding sometimes to syntactic units, sometimes to lines, of four-beat accentuals. And it is this persistence of traditional prosodies within the "non-numerical" convention of free verse which constitutes the true strength of "free verse," a strength which is not, as Hartman claims, its "flexibility" with respect to a poem's "content" but which lies in its inherent complexity and richness. In the best free verse what we hear is a loose medley of older prosodies; and these prosodies are present not primarily in order to "organically" augment "content" but for their own sake, as verbal music. They are present simply because, through overwhelming historical precedent, such music has come to make up an important— perhaps indispensable—element of that convention which we call "the poem."

In free-verse composition, then, much attention is paid to "prosody"; but it is not the kind of attention which Hartman describes above. Nor is it as sustained and detailed an attention as is paid to "prosody" during "metrical" composition, where the smallest unit of a poem, its every syllable, must receive consideration as to its sound and its location. Since "discovery" during poetic composition is most likely to be evidenced in those elements of a poem which receive the most attention, "prosodic" discovery is much more likely to occur during "metrical" composition than in the writing of free verse; and it is surely no accident that Hartman's prime example of discovery in free verse, "Valley Candle," does not evidence any significant prosodic discovery but exclusively structural discovery. Indeed, I am inclined to believe, with Paul Fussell, that free verse, deprived of such salient and insistent organizing principles as meter and end-rhyme, tends, in the fully realized poem, to seek compensatory higher organization at the structural level. As Herrnstein Smith has pointed out, the basis of structure is repetition. In good free-verse poems, we see the repetition which in metered composition takes the form of feet and syllabic count being transferred to larger units: to syntactic formulas of various lengths. Such repetition not only forms the very basis of "Valley Candle"; it is also in strong evidence throughout "First Practice," in the repetition of "And if" and, much more conspicuously, in the repetition of "He said," an important element in the poem's discovered structure, because the repetition does more than simply make the poem incantatory and stylize the rhetoric: the tone of "He said," as that clause recurs in an increasingly rich context, acquires greater complexity. From the poem's adult perspective, it becomes more and more accusatory; from the poem's boyhood perspective, it sounds at first earnest and later becomes the dulled, toneless, rote, "He-said-to-so-I-did" response of a hypnotized robot: prosodic discovery turns into structural discovery.

*   *   *   *

It has become a complacent and almost invidious truism that modernist and contemporary poetry are endlessly "experimental." The problem with the word "experimental" when applied to poems is that it is too apt to conjure up mere iconoclasm—a superficial flouting of convention. "Experimental" recalls the bad *vers libre* of, say, Carl Sandburg: the rebellious but coarsely indiscriminate hacking up of prose into lines. It recalls poetry without capital letters, without punctuation. It recalls any type of random, typographical vagary. But the fully achieved poem evidencing a "discovered" structure is, as we have seen, "experimental" in a far deeper and nontrivial sense of that word.

Hartman characterizes his own concept of "discovered" form as a reformulation in fresher language of the romantic concept of "organic" form. I cannot agree. I think that "discovered" poetic structure, both as developed by Hartman and as practiced by our poets, constitutes a pronounced *departure* from the romantics—that the differences between structural discovery and "organic form" are at least as significant as the similarities. It is true that when, in his *Preface*, Wordsworth insists that personifications must be deployed only when prompted by "passion," and that all good poetry is "the spontaneous overflow of powerful feelings," he is insisting, as Frost does, that for a poem to surprise or move the reader, it must authentically surprise or move its author during composition. But the kind of "discovery" which interests Wordsworth is limited. It is not structural or prosodic. It is exclusively rhetorical, a question of diction ("the language really used by men") and imagery ("colouring of imagination"). When Wordsworth writes, "The principal object . . . proposed in these Poems, was to choose incidents and situations from common life, and . . . to throw over them a certain colouring of imagination whereby ordinary things should be presented to the mind in an unusual aspect," he is strongly implying that we should read each of "these Poems" as if it were a prefabricated illusion, an accomplished effect with all the steps (the "evidence") by which the author achieved this effect erased so that the final illusion appears "spontaneous." Of course, it is important to Wordsworth (as it was to Coleridge) how poems come into being—by means of imagination rather than fancy—but for them the final product, no matter how reworked, is supposed to resemble a flash of vision. The process of poetic discovery is not to be part of the drama of a poem.

This need not surprise us. "Discovered structure," as we understand it, has virtually nothing to do with imagination as the romantics conceived it. Its origins are, if anything, antiromantic. It is not synthetic, it is analytic. It is a wholly modernist conception. Indeed, it is the main theme of virtually all our great modernist poems, from *The Four Quartets* to *Paterson* to "Thirteen Ways of Looking at a Blackbird." And if there is a difference between the "method" of discovered structure in modernist and in postmodern poems, it is only that the self-reflexivity of most modernist poetry was far more blatant than in most of the achieved poems of our contemporaries. Virtually all of the great modernist poems are, first and foremost, about poetry itself. In postmodern poems such as "Peppergrass" and "First Practice," on the other hand, we see the author attempting to turn his attention away from his own poem, toward experience. But because both poems' philosophy of composition—their method of invention—is entirely modernist, when we read them we still sense the drama through which these poems discovered their respective structures, clarifying their authors' elusive intimations into a definition of their intentionality.

7. The Paradox of Achieved Poetic Form

Perhaps the best approach to the profoundly paradoxical nature of achieved poetic form—how any fully achieved poem must, by its very nature, be deeply and inherently contradictory—would begin with a couple of remarks by Wallace Stevens, taken from "The Noble Rider and the Sound of Words." There Stevens characterizes what he calls "the nature of poetry" as "an interdependence of the imagination and reality as equals." And in that same essay he formulates his most memorable dictum: "It is a violence from within that protects us from a violence without. It is the imagination pressing back against the pressure of reality." All this sounds, of course, deceptively simple. We think, for example, of such familiar classroom specimens as Stevens's "The Snow Man" and of its trite interpretation. If there the "pressure of reality" is the absolute blankness of the inhuman world, the counterforce of imagination—the "violence from within"—results in whatever myths we project upon that blankness in order to comprehend it. Because we cannot comprehend the inhuman in anything but human terms, we hear "misery in the sound of the wind." To reduce this crude, schoolroom reading of Stevens to its lowest common denominator: so bleak, so wholly Other is "reality" that we insulate ourselves from it by means of fantasy. This interpretation is arguable, but only as far as it goes. For if we look hard at any good poem, we can begin to see that Stevens's almost mathematically abstract formulation of "the nature of poetry" is about much, much more than merely poetic imagery or our inclination to fantasize. We begin to see that, in the most highly elliptical way, Stevens is not only instructing us in the criticism of poetry: he is instructing us—perhaps not inadvertently warning us—about certain insidious artistic temptations, temptations which, as I will suggest later, coincide with the rise of modernism in poetry and its aftermath.

When Stevens claims that the "nature of poetry" is founded upon "an interdependence of the imagination and reality as equals," he is, in effect, suggesting that when we lose the ability or the will to distinguish between imagination and what he blithely calls "reality," when we can no longer distinguish between "fictional" experience and "historical" experience, we lose poetry. This may sound extreme. But if we think a little about the nature of poetic form, we can begin to see what Stevens is driving at. First of all, when Stevens refers to "imagination," he is referring not just to "images." He is referring to every aspect of poetic artifice—to prosody, to poetic structure, to every possible way in which a poem presumes to impose order upon "the nothing that is not there and the nothing that is." He is reminding us that in *every* respect achieved poetry is preeminently artificial, that it is "fictive" as distinguishable from "real" just as music is distinguishable from noise. More than that: he is reminding us that the nature of fiction is such that one might regard any good poem as a "violence" in precisely Stevens's sense of that word. A good poem so openly defies "reality" as to be, in itself, structurally inconsistent. To take the crudest example I can think of, the epistemology of a poem such as Keats's "Ode to a Nightingale" is a contradiction in terms. The protagonist is musing to himself, yet the utterance is somehow overheard. His inner life is supposedly a spontaneous process—a flowing of emotion—yet the poem is obviously the product of endless stitching and unstitching. And, finally, the most outrageous paradox: the subject matter of that ode is mostly subverbal, an immense welling up of longing, sadness, and vague desire, yet the poem is in words. In fact, the principal elements that comprise this poem's structure may be accounted for precisely *because* of the particular kinds of paradox which comprise that convention we call "lyric": first-person, present-tense narration in order to imitate spontaneous meditation; heavy reliance on imagery and rhythm to embody a content composed not so much of ideas as of "feelings." And note the paradoxical nature of our response to the poem. We accept the fiction of its convention, yet we do not respond to it as we would to an actual person—a friend, perhaps—who was confessing to us that he or she was depressed. We do not think,"I wish I could have helped poor Keats." Our response is rather like the passion we might feel at a basketball game where our team was losing. We might feel furious at the referee, and feel a loathing admiration for the opposing, seven-foot center; but we would not interrupt the game—go beyond its rules—to change its results. We would not shoot the referee or disable the opposing star any more than we would, or could, interfere with the characters in a play, a novel, or a poem. Indeed, to do so would be to misunderstand crucially the very nature of art. For we would be doing precisely what Stevens warns against. As measured by our behavior, "imagination" and "reality" could no longer be considered equals.

Consider for a moment how, in the analogy I am proposing, the rules which define the game of basketball as a *game* parallel principles of poetic form as *art*. In both "games," the timing, the boundaries, the protocol are entirely invented and then imposed upon "reality." Yet both games must be played by humans. To borrow a famous metaphor: both poetry and basketball are imaginary gardens populated by real toads. Both require their human players no less than do those players require the structure of the game. For what? For some sense of meaning. A well-constructed game is an arena which creates meaning. It is a place where good organization will usually win, where human character will make some difference in the outcome, and where beauty is possible. Yet note this paradox: although the game allows human nature to be expressed, the moment that human nature is expressed *outside* the rules of that game—suppose there is a fight among the players—our delight in the game ends. On the other hand, if there is not enough "pressure of reality" in the game—suppose neither team particularly wants to win— then it becomes trivial. Yeats expresses this epistemological paradox rather neatly, though a bit cryptically, in "Lapis Lazuli," a poem about aesthetic distance:

> All perform their tragic play,
> There struts Hamlet, there is Lear,
> That's Ophelia, that Cordelia;
> Yet they, should the last scene be there,
> The great stage curtain about to drop,
> If worthy their prominent part in the play,
> Do not break up their lines to weep.

Barbara Herrnstein Smith puts it equally well, if a bit more systematically, in *Poetic Closure*:

When we read a poem or hear it read, we are confronted by the performance of an act of speech, not the act itself. It is not "the speaker" who is speaking; . . . indeed, that speaker . . . may never have existed at all in the historical world.

Even when the poem is occasioned by the poet's actual experiences and is most nearly a transcription of his individual "voice," it remains, as a poem, only a *possible* utterance, what the poet *might* say. . . . the claim is not the same as that made upon us by one who addresses us directly, his discourse directly shaped by the pressures of an immediate or "historical" occasion. Both the poet, in composing the poem, and we, in responding to it, are aware of the distinction, and it controls both the form of his discourse and the nature of our response.

It has often been remarked that the tragic events in tragedies do not affect us as do the tragic events in our lives or in the lives of those we know or hear about. . . .

For the poem to have its characteristic effect, the representation must be sufficiently "realistic." That is, the literary artifact must create the illusion of being a historical utterance precisely to the extent that a play must create the illusion of being a historical action, which is to say *not completely*, the illusion is not to function as a deception . . . we might wonder, for example, if a spectator in a theatre who rushes on the stage to disarm the villain is any more naively or improperly deluded than the reader who believes, when he is reading Donne's "Holy Sonnets," that he is eavesdropping on the poet's private meditation.

Language, in poetry, is used mimetically. It is used, moreover, in a characteristic mimetic manner to suggest as vividly as possible (or necessary) that very historical context which it does *not*, in fact, possess.

It is impossible to explain the contradictory nature of a good poem better than this; but we can translate Herrnstein Smith's formulation into slightly different terms. She is arguing, in effect, that a successful poem must embody the following paradox: it must locate, in the particular, some sense of the general; it must present an experience which, despite its sense of specificity, is also, somehow, typical. This is certainly what Frost meant when he wrote, "Every poem is a new metaphor inside, or it is nothing." If a particular experience, when described in a poem, has no sense of typicality, it is meaningless. It stands for nothing. It refers to nothing beyond itself. It *is* only what it *is*, an incident which, because it is purely singular, is inconsequential.

It is the sense of implicit yet meant typicality which constitutes what is called "aesthetic distance," our sense that what we are beholding is art, not life, is illusion, not deception, that imagination is equally balanced against reality. Of course, too much sense of typicality without enough sense of the particular results, as we all know, in smug, mechanically structured, preachy poems. I suppose that Kilmer's infamous "Trees" constitutes as conveniently dead a horse of this ilk to flog as any—an extreme example of imagination unchecked by the pressure of reality: "I think that I shall never see / A poem lovely as a tree," and so on. The rigid prosody rules out the "reality" of the human voice, as well as the suppleness of authentic emotion. The sentiments and the easy generalizations which the poem toys with seem gratuitously imposed upon the poor trees—trees which have been hideously despoiled, which are as idealized and schematic as cartoons. In its imagery, in its prosody, in its structure, the poem is starved for reality. Of course, Kilmer would contend that he was expressing "reality" as he perceived it. But the louder he insisted, the more emphatically would he be making Stevens's very point: the moment we lose the ability to distinguish between fiction and history, we can no longer distinguish between what is trite and what is fresh. "Trees," like the Georgian poetry which Pound and Eliot so justifiably mocked, consists of a set of frilly rhetorical manners which is empty: empty but—*and this is the point*—its practitioners *do not know* that it is empty. They mistake their manners for reality itself. Stevens's brilliant poem "The Man on the Dump" is about just this slippage into complacency. It ends with the image of the poet sitting on a dump composed of all the dead images that make up his culture, his literary inheritance, his very environment. The poet is beating a tin can and dreaming of finding something fresh and original—"the truth"—under all the clichés and the cultural dreck:

> Is it to sit among mattresses of the dead
> Bottles, pots, shoes and grass and murmur *aptest eve*:
> Is it to hear the blatter of grackles and say
> *Invisible priest*; is it to eject, to pull
> The day to pieces and cry *stanza my stone*?
> Where was it one first heard of the truth? The the.

In his mocking of phrasing like "aptest eve," "Invisible priest," and "stanza my stone," Stevens is mocking poetry that is, as

Williams so nicely put it, "stale, stale as literature." But "The Man on the Dump" could just as easily be taken as a criticism of where the assumptions of modernism would ultimately lead by a kind of *reverse* logic, how modernism itself, for all its insistence on "freshness," could ultimately produce a confusion of "fiction" and "history" just as absolute and emasculating as that which lies behind the bombastic death-rattles of the Georgians. For example, in the so-called "postmodernist" mode—in the figure of a poet like John Ashbery—we see a man sitting on the dump and very urbanely rearranging the trash into curious and parodic designs. Like Kilmer, Ashbery would contend that he was expressing the truth as he saw it; but his argument on behalf of his epistemology would, unlike Kilmer's, *deliberately* undermine distinctions between fiction and history.

Ashbery would contend that there is nothing *but* the dump, that there is no important difference between the smell of dinner in the kitchen and a football game on television, that both are equally "real," that in a media-saturated environment like ours, distinctions between the "real" and the "fictional" break down. Indeed, he would contend that if art is to be true to "reality" it must be like his: it must systematically break down such distinctions as "imagination" versus "reality."

Ashbery's poems are demonstrations of this epistemology—dump-shaped heaps of images, scraps of conversation, literature, all forms of discourse, recapitulating that daily melange of fantasy, media event, and trivial happening which makes up the texture of our experience. But such poetry, like basketball without the score being kept, is rather dull. Never in Ashbery's poems do we feel the seriousness of life, that the play is, as Frost would put it, "for mortal stakes."

Poetry as a dump of images: the idea is not that new. *The Waste Land* follows just such a strategy. Indeed, in the elegant frittering of an Ashbery, what we see is the logic of modernism carried to its extreme, come full circle. As we know, the early battles of the modernists were waged in order to restore precisely that equal balance of "imagination" and "reality" so absent in the Georgians. Such modernist catchphrases as "direct treatment of the thing" and "no ideas but in things" are demands that poetic form allow a greater impingement of "reality," the freshness of "the the." This is why, in the great modernist poems, we find traditional form—"stale literature" as it were—discarded in favor of experiments in analogical form: poems with the shapes of "real" things, poems as ideograms, as collages, as sibylline fragments, as string quartets, as human speech with actual "sentence sounds," as the individual mind in the very process of fiction-making. The main drift of poetry in the postmodern era has merely been to extend the range of formal analogues so as to include more personal types of discourse such as "confession" and "conversation." But, as I have already suggested in my remarks about Ashbery, the consequences of allowing the "pressure of reality" to impinge too heavily on poetic form ultimately undermine, in a different way, poetry itself. What is called "the fallacy of imitative form"—the fallacious notion that, for example, the best way to write about boredom is to be boring—is a uniquely modern invention. The more a poem imitates something nonliterary—for example, talk—the harder it is to turn the discourse into art. This is why open-form poetry is often so sloppy, so self-indulgently garrulous. As Herrnstein Smith would put it, what happens when the fallacy of imitative form is committed is that what should be "illusion" tends toward "deception." We hear only the pathetic, tiresome voices of real people struggling in the swelter of their lives. Whereas Kilmer's "Trees" is sterile by virtue of too *much* aesthetic distance, bad free-verse confession is dull for absence of it. Indeed, when the poet strives to make a myth of his personal life, the moment that the distinction between illusion and deception is blurred, the poetry becomes a form of written insanity: what had been a tense game erupts into a fight, often with mortal consequences—a fight which we watch with horror. As we read a book like Anne Sexton's *The Awful Rowing Toward God*, we are put very much in the position of Herrnstein Smith's naive reader who would rush on stage to disarm the poet from destroying herself. We remember the totally unforgivable way in which, before Sexton's death, her agent would market her performance: by assuring the sponsor that, somewhere in her reading, she was guaranteed to cry. I would like, though, to explore this second extreme a little further. For despite the risks of a personal poetry, I believe that the main task given the postmodern poet continues to be to elaborate the myths of the individual self as it dons mask after mask of language in its life-long, continuous quest for a valid style—for integrity in the face of that "violence without."

*   *   *   *

I do not believe that, as Cervantes alleges, Don Quixote's imagination went out of control because Quixote had read too many romances. To be sure, romances gave his imagination a vocabulary to play with—a chivalric one—but it was not the stories themselves, it was his *saying* their vocabulary, his acting it, that made it come too true—could turn the frumpy, garlic-breathed Dulcinea into a lady, a windmill into some eternal, ever-impudent adversary. Think of the way our own words, especially words uttered under pressure, shake us, become little mythologies which can change us. Think, for example, of how we are bodily changed when, facing somebody who is the source of our grievance, we *say* our anger. Think of "I love you," how it changes us slightly the first time we say it. And how hard to unsay it—the peculiar, sticky way in which we commit ourselves to our words—how it injures us, almost, to call them back. William Stafford is squarely tackling these matters when, in "Report from a Far Place," speaking of what he calls "these word things," he warns, "Be careful, though: they / burn, or don't burn, in their own / strange way, when you say them." Not words: word-*things*. Our words carry the world into us. And this is why poetry, like prayer, will never die out. It will always be the darkest, subtlest, most intrinsic and stubbornly enduring human art, so fundamental is the level at which our tongue touches us: our meant words, what people have to warm their hands by when they have nothing left, when every roof is gone. And the mythologies we make with our words are not so much "about" as they are *of* ourselves: "I'm shy." "I'm bitter with my job." "My heart is broken." "I'm in a good mood today." Each of these prophecies is, by virtue of its simply being uttered, to some extent self-fulfilling.

It is because of this blood tie we have with our words—their mythologizing power—that the stakes in a personal poetry are so high. Such poetry is dangerous because it can change us; yet it is just as necessary as it is dangerous, because it is the art that most deeply defines us. As Richard Hugo put it in his "Letter to Mayo from Missoula," "lines are really the veins of men / whether men know it or not. And if the saying of it / is, as Stafford says, a lonely thing, it is also / the gritty. . . ." What a hard task Hugo has set for us. To be any good, lines must be the poet's veins. But they must, simultaneously, achieve aesthetic distance. That is the paradox. The poet must be, as Whitman said of himself in *Song of Myself*, "both in and out of the game." The same voice in the same poem must be able, one moment, to ask of itself, "Who goes there, hankering, gross, mystical, nude?" and at the next moment to seem to swoon in erotic ecstasy, to seem to lose self-consciousness almost entirely. The voice, in its very stances, must contradict itself at every turn. We recall what Herrnstein Smith said: "A poem must suggest that very historical context which it does *not* in fact possess." In the case of a personal poetry, we might turn this dictum around. We might better say: "The poem should try to transcend, to deny that very historical context which it *does*, in fact, possess." If it cannot, it commits the fallacy of imitative form. Which is to say that it functions merely as a "deception." A good example of such a poem would be John Logan's "Three Moves," which appears in Poulin's *Contemporary American Poetry*. The poem, which resembles a letter, is directed to a "you" who is probably the reader, and it is signed "Seattle, April 1965."

> Three moves in six months and I remain
> the same.
> Two homes made two friends.
> The third leaves me with myself again.
> (We hardly speak.)
> Here I am with tame ducks
> and my neighbor's boats,
> only this electric heat
> against the April damp.
> I have a friend named Frank—
> The only one who ever dares to call
> and ask me, "How's your soul?"
> I hadn't thought about it for a while,
> and was ashamed to say I didn't know.
> I have no priest for now.
> Who
> will forgive me then. Will you?
> Tame birds and my neighbors' boats.

The ducks honk about the floats. . .
They walk dead drunk onto the land and grounds,
iridescent blue and black and green and brown.
They live on swill
our aged houseboats spill.
But still they are beautiful.
Look! The duck with its unlikely beak
has stopped to pick
and pull
at the potted daffodil.
Then again they sway home
to dream
bright gardens of fish in the early night.
Oh these ducks are all right.
They will survive.
But I am sorry I do not often see them climb.
Poor sons-a-bitching ducks.
You're all fucked up.
What do you do that for?
Why don't you hover near the sun anymore?
Afraid you'll melt?
These foolish ducks lack a sense of guilt,
and so all their multi-thousand-mile range
is too short for the hope of change.

I must confess that this poem seems to me little more than a plea for sympathy thrown out like a note in a bottle for the world to find. Why does the poem subsist at such a low level? Because in it imagination and reality are not in equal opposition. The myth of the poem's words as well as its form is indistinguishable from the reality of the poet's life, and the poet cannot tell the difference. As a result, the poem lacks what I think of as "plot." What do I mean by plot? To answer this question, let us look at a second, more successful Logan poem, "Lines on His Birthday":

I was born on a street named Joy
of which I remember nothing,
but since I was a boy
I've looked for its lost turning.
Still I seem to hear my mother's cry
echo in the street of joy.
She was sick as Ruth for home
when I was born. My birth
took away my father's wife

and left me half
my life. Christ will my remorse
be less when my father's dead?
Or more. As Lincoln's minister of war
kept the body of his infant boy
in a silver coffin on his desk,
so I keep
in a small heirloom box of teak
the picture of my living father.
Or perhaps it is an image of myself
dead in the box she held?
I know her milk like ivory blood
still runs in my thick veins
and still leaves in me an almost
lickerish taste for ghosts:
my mother's wan face,
full brown hair, the mammoth breast
death cuts off at the bone—
to which she draws her bow
again, brazen Amazon,
and aiming deadly as a saint
shoots her barb
of guilt into my game heart.

Why is this poem so much better than "Three Moves"? First, at every point we are aware of a tension between the poet's somewhat artificial prosody and allegorizing, on the one hand, and the terrible facts of his life, on the other. The more we become aware of this tension, the more we realize that the poem's real plot is not the story of the poet's grief-filled past, per se, a story, in any case, only hinted at and never fully told. The poem's real plot is the way in which the speaker is struggling, as we all do, to explain his sorrow by means of some mythology or other, some little, summarizing song. The main plot of the poem, then, is the speaker's struggle *in the poem*. We are moved not so much by Logan's sorrow as by the "game" way he sets about making a myth of it, a myth replete with its lost street named "Joy," the joy of undifferentiated, prenatal existence, perhaps; but, equally possible, the longed-for "joy" of being unborn. The poem, then, is not so much about *what* Logan knows as it is a dramatization of *how* we experiment with different ways of knowing about knowing. It is, as Stevens would put it, a "poem of the mind in the act of finding what will suffice." The aesthetic distance, then, that enables "Lines on His Birthday" to transcend its ostensible status of being merely a personal utterance arises from our sense that the speaker not only knows what he is doing *but wants us to know that he knows.* The poem's very playfulness alerts us of this. Poetic form—such tactfully displayed self-consciousness in terms of artifice—is like a game: a subtle contract with the reader.

A still better poem about personal mythmaking is Richard Hugo's famous "Degrees of Gray in Philipsburg." If we know much about Hugo's life, we know that the poem is, in large part, about the temptation by Hugo to deliberately ruin his life through heavy drinking and through systematic dwelling on an unhappy childhood, in order to get material for poems, to turn that inner sense of failure which he had obsessively, time and time again, mythologized in the failed landscapes so many of his poems depict into a self-fulfilling prophecy. It is about the temptation, as Hugo put it once, to confuse "the man and the mask." But we need not know any of this to like the poem, for it transcends the particular:

> You might come here Sunday on a whim.
> Say your life broke down. The last good kiss
> you had was years ago. You walk these streets
> laid out by the insane, past hotels
> that didn't last, bars that did, the tortured try
> of local drivers to accelerate their lives.
> Only churches are kept up. The jail
> turned 70 this year. The only prisoner
> is always in, not knowing what he's done.
>
> The principal supporting business now
> is rage. Hatred of the various grays
> the mountain sends, hatred of the mill,
> The Silver Bill repeal, the best liked girls
> who leave each year for Butte. One good
> restaurant and bars can't wipe the boredom out.
> The 1907 boom, eight going silver mines,
> a dance floor built on springs—
> all memory resolves itself in gaze,
> in panoramic green you know the cattle eat
> or two stacks high above the town,
> two dead kilns, the huge mill in collapse
> for fifty years that won't fall finally down.

Isn't this your life? That ancient kiss
still burning out your eyes? Isn't this defeat
so accurate, the church bell simply seems
a pure announcement: ring and no one comes?
Don't empty houses ring? Are magnesium
and scorn sufficient to support a town,
not just Philipsburg, but towns
of towering blondes, good jazz and booze
the world will never let you have
until the town you came from dies inside?

Say no to yourself. The old man, twenty
when the jail was built, still laughs
although his lips collapse. Someday soon,
he says, I'll go to sleep and not wake up.
You tell him no. You're talking to yourself.
The car that brought you here still runs.
The money you buy lunch with,
no matter where it's mined, is silver
and the girl who serves you food
is slender and her red hair lights the wall.

Ultimately, it is in its extraordinary (though implicit) self-consciousness that "Degrees of Gray" preserves that characteristic which Herrnstein Smith so rightly insists distinguishes "illusion" from "deception"—the sense of being only a "possible" utterance. Some of the hypothetical quality of the poem derives from its deployment of a "you" instead of an "I." "You," as we know, can become a mechanical way of asserting aesthetic distance—a sense of typicality—in poems which should be testimonial. Here, however, "you" is appropriate because the whole poem is proffered not as history but as a hypothesis: if one's life broke down, then one might create a myth like this one. Hugo goes on to spin a myth, as usual in terms of a derelict landscape; and because this myth is his life-long obsession and he is all too good at mythmaking, his description has great force. We watch the "you" gradually becoming so carried away with his own creation that he sings himself to the brink of total belief—"Isn't this your life?"—whereupon, recognizing the danger of confusing his historical life with his mythologized version of it, he repudiates the myth (though he has to tear himself away), lest he actually allow himself, in the service of a fiction, to "break down."

Indeed, one of the reasons why "Degrees of Gray" rings so true is because it is so dangerous. For who *is* the speaking "you"? Is it Hugo talking to his failing persona? Is it Hugo's persona talking to himself? Or is it Hugo talking to himself? As this poem quite consciously dramatizes in the very indefiniteness of its ruling pronoun, the confusion of an author's identity with that of his persona can be insidious, and the dangers of such a confusion can be as real as the question of whether "your life broke down" or you only "say" it did. "Degrees of Gray" nakedly confronts this paradox and wins: it preserves aesthetic distance while demonstrating how high are the stakes in a personal poetry, how in an irredeemably secular world, any of the secular myths with which an individual would invest his self is an all-too-plausible temptation into total belief, into madness.

It is this issue—an issue which first appears two hundred years ago and finds its early full expression in Whitman's *Song of Myself* and in Wordsworth's *Prelude*—that continues to define the main line of development in our poetry: how the isolate self in a secular world, without recourse to the easy, extrinsic authority of priest or psychiatrist, must rely on its own ingenuity, on sheer force of character, to stay sane— must again and again impose a song, a brief order of imagination, upon a violent reality; how, paradoxically, though the singer sings in order to stay sane, he must shun the solipsistic madness of total belief in his own song; how, finally, the only way to do this is through imagination—which is nothing less than the power to discover form.

These issues are the subject of Stephen Dunn's "The Routine Things Around The House," a poem about aesthetic distance, about where to stop, about finding the precise "place" where the violence within meets, on equal terms, the violence without, a poem whose very dialectic, then, dramatizes the redemptive power of imagination, of achieved poetic form.

> When mother died
> I thought: now I'll have a death poem.
> That was unforgivable
>
> yet I've since forgiven myself
> as sons are able to do
> who've been loved by their mothers.

I stared into the coffin
knowing how long she'd live,
how many lifetimes there are

in the sweet revisions of memory.
It's hard to know exactly
how we ease ourselves back from sadness,

but I remembered when I was twelve,
1951, before the world
unbuttoned its blouse.

I had asked my mother (I was trembling)
if I could see her breasts
and she took me into her room

without embarrassment or coyness
and I stared at them,
afraid to ask for more.

Now, years later, someone tells me
Cancers who've never had mother love
are doomed and I, a Cancer,

feel blessed again. What luck
to have had a mother
who showed me her breasts

when girls my age were developing
their separate countries,
what luck

she didn't doom me
with too much or too little.
Had I asked to touch,

perhaps to suck them,
what would she have done?
Mother, dead woman

who I think permits me
to love women easily,
this poem

is dedicated to where
we stopped, to the incompleteness
that was sufficient

and to how you buttoned up,
began doing the routine things
around the house.

I do not think there is, among our poets, a voice more intimate than Dunn's. Note, though, that for all its daring intimacy, we know that we are in the presence of art. The poem *almost* makes us feel embarrassed, but not quite. It tightropes the perfect balance between illusion and deception. Its degree of concealment is just right. Note, for example, how tactfully the poem poses its theme at the very beginning, in the words "unforgivable" and "forgiven." The issues which the poem is going to tackle are broad aesthetic ones, yet they are posed in authentically personal terms. We realize immediately that the poem we are reading is going to be that very "unforgivable" yet perhaps "forgivable" death poem which Dunn had mentioned, that this poem is going to be a self-conscious dramatization of the potentially deceptive, exploitive way in which *any* writer is tempted to use his experience. We begin to realize that this poem *is* in its way almost as dangerous as the Hugo poem, and that both are in a sense experiments in how to "forgive" the "unforgivable" by means of poetry, through form. And as we become aware that the mother in Dunn's poem, like the waitress who serves the protagonist "food" at the end of "Degrees of Gray," is a muse figure—that it is she who has initiated the speaker into life's three central mysteries, into birth, sex, and death—we begin to sense, barely under the surface, a kind of suppressed allegory, that the poem is in part self-reflexive. We marvel at how absolutely dual the muse figure is. How perfectly she embodies that reconciliation of opposites which, according to Stevens, following Coleridge, is intrinsic to the nature of poetry. She embodies at once the unforgivable pressure of reality which could, as the speaker says, "doom me," yet she also embodies the potentiality for "sweet revisions," for a form, here presented as a memory, by which "we ease ourselves back from sadness," a form which, because it knows when to "button up," is salvational: it dooms one neither with too much nor too little. "This poem," Dunn concludes, "is dedicated to where we stopped." On the literal level, "where we stopped" refers both to Dunn's mother's death and to her buttoning up. Although Dunn has not for an instant broken up the lines to weep, this dedication is a gracious gesture, ever so "forgivable." He has offered his dead mother the most judicious praise. He has truly honored her. He has put the quality of his poem, his technique, on the line as an explicit test of his sincerity, so that on both the literal *and* the figurative level the dedication is to the muse. She, in her mysterious doubleness, has permitted him to write this poem, a poem which is, as all achieved poems must to some extent *but only to some extent* be, about the discovery of its own form: about itself.

III

The Use of Poetry

There were ten thousand thousand fruit to touch,
Cherish in hand, lift down, and not let fall.
For all
That struck the earth,
No matter if not bruised or spiked with stubble,
Went surely to the cider-apple heap
As of no worth.

—Robert Frost

8. Poetry and Mathematics

One of the most evocative things that Paul Valéry ever said was that he wished his poems to have "the solidity of certain pages of algebra." As a poet who has been an amateur mathematician and who was for three years a teacher of advanced high school mathematics and calculus, I immediately recognize what Valéry is talking about. Passages of algebra, indented and breaking free from prose text, visually resemble passages of poetry, as if, out of the plodding welter of expository prose and fastidious explanation, some higher, more intense language had suddenly burst forth like a pure aria issuing from recitative—for example, the elementary proof by "mathematical induction" that, starting with the integer 1, the sum of the first n odd integers is the square of n:

$$\sum_{p=1}^{n} (2p - 1) = n^2 \Rightarrow \sum_{p=1}^{n+1}(2p - 1) =$$

$$\sum_{p=1}^{n} (2p - 1) + [2(n + 1) - 1] = n^2 + 2n + 1 = (n + 1)^2.$$

When I was much younger, such flourishes of nomenclature seemed to me glamorous, abstruse, runic, and eternal, everything which, as an undergraduate poet laboring at wheezing translations from French symbolist poems, I knew that a poem should be—a hermitage of pure mind to which one could retreat from the ugly, inconvenient, and merely provisional aspects of sublunary life. Of course, all analogies limp. Mathematics cannot be a "pure aria." Of all our written languages, it is the most visual, the least oral, the language closest to silence. The first equation above, read aloud, is toneless and cumbersome, lacking the beautifully abbreviated quality of its graph: "The sum of the first p odd integers, from 1 through n, equals n squared." But the pithiness, the extreme condensation of the formula, was—still is—immensely appealing. Here was concentrated truth, applicable perhaps to many situations but, like a tiny, powerful, aphoristic poem, readily possessable and portable. When I was around twenty-six, teaching calculus to five students who were smarter enough than I was to make teaching them intimidating, I tried, in a poem, to fix some of the aesthetic allure of pages of double and triple integrals:

Integrals

> Erect, arched in disdain,
> the integrals drift from left
> across white windless pages
> to the right,
> serene as swans.

> Tall,
> beautiful seen from afar
> on the wavering water, each
> curves with the balanced severity
> of a fine tool weighed in the palm.

> Gaining energy now, they
> break into a canter—stallions
> bobbing the great crests of their manes.
> No one suspects their power
> who has not seen them rampage.
>   Like bulldozers, they build
> by adding
>   dirt to dirt to stumps added
>   to boulders to broken glass added
>   to live trees by the roots added
> to hillsides, to whole
> housing developments
>   that roll, foaming before them,
> the tumbling end of a broken wave
> in one mangled sum: dandelions, old
> beer-cans and broken
> windows—gravestones all
> rolled into one.

> Yes, with the use of tables
> integration is as easy as that:

the mere squeeze of a trigger, no
second thought. The swans
cannot feel the pain
it happens so fast.

Swans, liberated from the utilitarian charts of the Chemical
Rubber Company's 14th edition of *Standard Mathematical Tables*,
like the proof sketched earlier, constitute the aspect of mathematics which Valéry, with his devotion to "poésie pure,"
would have especially liked. The proof is "pure" mathematics,
mathematics unapplied. It is elegantly tautological: mathematical sentences that are about nothing except other mathematical sentences, just as some poems can be about poetry,
which is to say, about themselves.

The raison d'être of mathematics is not, however, primarily
aesthetic. Number is the most practical language which human beings have devised by which to orient themselves
within the physical dimensions of the world and to measure
that world. Valéry's attraction to "purity" in "pages of algebra" and in poetry is overrefined, precious. His famous
analogy between poetry and dance—that poetry is to prose
as dance is to walking, because poetry uses words as a dancer
uses steps, as ends in themselves, whereas prose uses words
as a walker uses steps, as means to an end, as mere transpor-
tation—trivializes poetry, reducing it to merely pretty language, equivalent to an entirely "pure" mathematics concerned only with elegant proofs of its own consistency. But
the function of poetry, like the function of mathematics, is
measurement; and "measurement" presumes that there is
something to measure. What, then, does a good poem attempt to measure? And how seriously can analogies between
poems and "certain pages of algebra" be drawn? Are such
analogies fun but trivial? To get at answers to these questions,
let us consider some of the poetry of Wallace Stevens.

Stevens was by far the most mathematically sophisticated of
recent American poets. His poems regularly allude to mathematical ideas, affectionately imitate mathematical demonstrations, and apply language "mathematically" to the world. The
most obviously mathematical poem of Stevens is "Anecdote of
the Jar":

I placed a jar in Tennessee,

And round it was, upon a hill.
It made the slovenly wilderness
Surround that hill.

The wilderness rose up to it,
And sprawled around, no longer wild.
The jar was round upon the ground
And tall and of a port in air.

It took dominion everywhere.
The jar was gray and bare.
It did not give of bird or bush,
Like nothing else in Tennessee.

Here, the jar is the origin of a Cartesian coordinate system imposed upon the "wilderness" of a physical world unmapped in human terms.[1] Stevens is even careful to propose a vertical "z"-coordinate: the jar was "tall and of a port in air." And he is careful to remind us that the terms being imposed upon this "wilderness" are, like lines and points, wholly imaginary, wholly ideal, that this "jar" was "the only thing" in Tennessee which "did not give of bird or bush."

"Anecdote of the Jar" does not actually set out to measure anything in particular. It is about the conditions for measurement of "wilderness." Measurement is done, Stevens tells us, by imposing upon the world constructions of the imagination, ideal structures, terms which can only be sustained through something akin to Coleridge's "willing suspension of disbelief for the moment, which constitutes poetic faith." This identical phrase could be used to describe exactly the kind of assumption—the kind of "faith"—which is the basis of every mathematical construction, a construction which begins with the implicit if not the explicit injunction "Let us assume that . . . ."[2] But what does poetry, when at its best, actually measure? Stevens's "Sea Surface Full of Clouds" is a demonstration constructed expressly to address this question. The first two of the poem's five sections read as follows:

1. Is it an accident or characteristic of Stevens's wit and attention to minutiae that the round mouth of the jar just happens to resemble the zero at the origin of a Cartesian coordinate system and the letter "o" of "origin"?
2. In Stevens's "Connoisseur of Chaos" the passage "The pensive man . . . He sees that eagle float / For which the intricate Alps are a single nest" alludes to the suspension of disbelief which allows us to view a line as both one continuum ("single nest") and as a set of discrete points (the separate peaks of "Alps").

I

In that November off Tehuantepec,
The slopping of the sea grew still one night
And in the morning summer hued the deck

And made one think of rosy chocolate
And gilt umbrellas. Paradisal green
Gave suavity to the perplexed machine

Of ocean, which like limpid water lay.
Who, then, in that ambrosial latitude
Out of the light evolved the moving blooms,

Who, then, evolved the sea-blooms from the clouds
Diffusing balm in that Pacific calm?
C'était mon enfant, mon bijou, mon âme.

The sea-clouds whitened far below the calm
And moved, as blooms, in the swimming green
And in its watery radiance, while the hue

Of heaven in an antique reflection rolled
Round those flotillas. And sometimes the sea
Poured brilliant iris on the glistening blue.

II

In that November off Tehuantepec
The slopping of the sea grew still one night.
And breakfast jelly yellow streaked the deck

And made one think of chop-house chocolate
And sham umbrellas. And a sham-like green
Capped summer-seeming on the tense machine

Of ocean, which in sinister flatness lay.
Who, then, beheld the rising of the clouds
That strode submerged in that malevolent sheen,

Who saw the mortal massives of the blooms
Of water moving on the water-floor?
C'était mon frère du ciel, ma vie, mon or.

The gongs rang loudly as the windy booms
Hoo-hooed it in the darkened ocean-blooms.
The gongs grew still. And then blue heaven spread

Its crystalline pendentives on the sea
And the macabre of the water-glooms
In an enormous undulation fled.

In each of the five sections, certain elements of the scene—
"chocolate," "umbrellas," "green," "machine," "blooms," and
"clouds"—oriented with respect to "the deck"—are held as
invariants in a changing light, first a "morning summer" hue,
next a "streaked" "breakfast jelly yellow," next a "patterned"
"pale silver," then a "mallow morning," and, finally, "The
day . . . bowing and voluble." Each "light" projects a different atmosphere. Or, rather, each set of terms introducing the
"light" determines another set of terms which, in turn, determines the distinctive ambience of each section, each "scene"—
an ambience which, though believable, is conspicuously synthetic in much the same way that Eliot, in "Tradition and
the Individual Talent," suggests, with his metaphor drawn
from chemistry, that "art-emotion" is synthetic. When terms
such as "rosy chocolate," "gilt umbrellas," "Paradisal green,"
"suavity," "perplexed," and "machine" are put together, they
so mutually react, so color one another, that they form something new, a combination in which none of them retains
its original properties: they form not a mixture but a new
compound. Eliot's metaphor is more than satisfactory. It
implicitly portrays the poet as a word-scientist conducting,
in the laboratory of the poem, an experiment. We know, too,
that behind Eliot's metaphor lies the *symboliste* enthrallment
with the synthetic and with the ideal, Mallarmé's professed
intent to synthesize the "flower absent from all bouquets."
But if we make the short leap from a chemical metaphor to
a mathematical one, we find an analogue which may be as satisfying as Eliot's; we find, in fact, that Eliot's analogy, for all its
virtues, has obscured some other illuminating connections.
We might think of the invariant structure of "chocolate,"
"umbrellas," "green," "machine," "blooms," and "clouds"
as akin to coefficients in a polynomial, $f(x)$, of the form
$a_n x^n + a_{n-1} x^{n-1} + \ldots + a_1 x + a_0$ in which the variable, x, the deck,
can assume a different value or "light" in each section, so that
each section rather playfully, as if in demonstration, yields a
different value for $f(x)$ as each new "light" is substituted for x.
In this poem, the "value," instead of being numerical, is aesthetic—a mood, a flavor, a feeling-tone, an intimation of

something impalpable yet recognizable; for just as number is a specialized language that has evolved to express quantifiable values, poetry is the specialized language that has evolved to express synthetically otherwise inexpressible aesthetic values and experiences.

We might entertain a different mathematical analogy: the "deck" in each section is analogous to the Cartesian coordinate system in two dimensions; "chocolate," "umbrellas," "green," "machine," "blooms," and "clouds" are points—the vertices of some hexagonal geometrical figure composed of vectors mapped onto the plane. This hexagonal figure seems to change in each section, as the "deck," the axes in each section, are translated or rotated or altered in scale. But actually the polygon remains invariant: only the axes with respect to which the polygon is oriented and scaled are transformed. The poem, like a mathematical demonstration, escorts us through a sequence of linear transformations. Moreover, like a mathematical demonstration, in each of its steps it succeeds, through its specialized language, in expressing "something" which, without this language, would have remained inexpressible and, because it was inexpressible, scarcely perceptible at all. It is this issue of "inexpressibility" which should enable us to appreciate fully the analogy between poetry and mathematics and how serious this analogy might be. Without mathematics, how would we describe the orbit of a planet? As "round"? As an "oval" path? How close to looking like a circle? How "eccentric"? Without the quadratic equations that graph an ellipse, we are reduced to clumsy guesses, incredibly crude linguistic approximations. The mathematical formula for the ellipse, on the other hand, can yield us the *precise* shape. It is the *only* way to express that shape. Similarly, without mathematics, how would we express the behavior of a falling object? All we could say was that it goes "faster and faster and faster." But how "fast" does it go "faster"? Only a differential equation can express this precisely and meaningfully. "Acceleration" can be measured only in mathematical terms. Indeed, the entire concept of "acceleration" is meaningful only in mathematical terms.

Is there an analogous "something" that can be expressed precisely—be measured—only by means of the specialized terms of poetry? I think so. And I think that the mysteriously impalpable moods and changes of light synthesized in each section of "Sea Surface Full of Clouds"—moods which, though seemingly ineffable, we recognize through the language of the poem—demonstrate the specialized capacity of poetic language, like mathematical language, to measure accurately and thereby to find names for areas of experience which would otherwise have eluded us. But even as I suggest this, I am poignantly aware that I cannot prove it. The poem must serve as its own demonstration. Either the reader is overcome with recognition of what had hitherto seemed insufficiently expressed, or the reader is left cold. Auden puts rather neatly this "inexpressibility" theorem of poetry, linking it with the very function of poetry itself, in the prologue to *The Sea and the Mirror*:

> Well, who in his own backyard
> Has not opened his heart to the smiling
> Secret he cannot quote?
> Which goes to show that the Bard
> Was sober when he wrote

Pope put a similar idea into somewhat more modest terms: "True wit is Nature to advantage dressed, / What oft was thought, but ne'er so well expressed." One can attempt to explicate each section of "Sea Surface Full of Clouds," to apply "interpretation" as a means of convincing the skeptical reader that there is "something" recognizable being measured and named by each section, "something" which might be mutually acknowledged with a nod or perhaps a sharp intake of breath or a bristling of the pores—by a *frisson*. But if the poem cannot accomplish this by itself—if it cannot be its own demonstration—extrinsic attempts at demonstration will never suffice, but will remain prime targets, ludicrous sitting ducks, to be coolly picked off by the poststructuralist critics. And so I will leave "Sea Surface Full of Clouds" undisturbed, trusting that it is its own sufficient testimony.

Here the analogy between poetry and mathematics is weakest. Many kinds of measurement of physical phenomena can be empirically verified at will, and each remeasurement will yield, for public verification, approximately the same numbers. The reader-response of an individual to a literary work, however, as we are often reminded in the current critical climate, can never be susceptible to such ready verification, no matter how historically, ethnically, geographically, and linguistically homogeneous the audience. Nevertheless, the entire enterprise of poetry—of literature—must operate on the assumption of commonality, of shared familiarity with literary convention. It must operate on the assumption that a reasonably sophisticated audience will derive experiences approximately congruent enough from reading the same text that these experiences are, at least partially, communicable, and that readers of the same text can therefore use the terms of that text in order to discuss among themselves, with improved precision, their own experiences. Even "Sea Surface Full of Clouds," though seemingly untranslatable, can function this way, as well as in the private way in which Auden suggests. For example, it is easy to imagine a situation in which two people are on a cruise, the sun is rising, and one person remarks to the other, "This scene reminds me of the opening section of Stevens's 'Sea Surface Full of Clouds.' Stevens captured the mood, the light, exactly." The poem's own terms are so self-sufficient that, because they *cannot* be translated, they *need not* be. Indeed, on this very untranslatability is founded the public utility of art. Terms which first come to light in art, expressing something which had hitherto been insufficiently expressed, create their own community of those who recognize what the terms mean, what the terms refer to. The new terms then become, for that audience, a shared language which supplements and more finely differentiates the languages which they had started out with. Occasionally, terms originating in works of art will pass entirely into the domain of public language, of language which does not require such specific initiation, terms, for example, like "Babbitt" and "Scrooge."

The terms in literary works are, of course, far less universally acknowledged than the truly international language of number; but both languages clearly depend upon a suspension of disbelief. This suspension of disbelief—the implicit "Let us assume . . ." which makes mathematics possible—is the convention (the mathematical term might be the "axiom") which makes extrapolation possible to begin with, leading toward any number of constructions—an "algebra," a number system, a "geometry." The literary equivalent to a word like "algebra" would be the name of a genre—poetry, the novel, biography, and so on—which is the name of nothing more than a highly evolved convention. When somebody asks me,

"What is a poem?," I know the answer. A poem is a convention—a highly artificial one. Although this answer usually disappoints the questioner, it implicitly describes how and even why poets write; for our sense of what a poem is and what it is for is nothing if not the sum of our memories of all the poems we have ever seriously studied or used, a list including styles as various as those of Pope and Creeley, the *Beowulf* poet and Mallarmé—what Eliot accurately characterized as The Tradition. Whenever we set out to write, we have somewhere in mind a sense of how our language should call attention to itself so as to qualify as "poetry" and to belong to the tradition—a sense rather like one which children have when, hearing "Once upon a time . . .," they know that this opening will be followed by "there was a . . .," and that a story will unfold.

It is self-evident that conventions are never static. They are always being added onto at the margins. They evolve layer by layer, by accretions. All the layers are remembered simultaneously. Some layers fall into neglect or disrepute but may later, like the poetry of Donne, be excavated and restored to prominence, reincorporated into the most recent, hybrid, surface layer. It is during transitional periods, when a genre, poetry, is receiving a new layer or when an older, inner layer is being rediscovered, that the architects of the change will often defend their proposed alterations by trying to argue that one element or another of the convention is somehow "functional"—for example, Coleridge's defense of "metre" as providing a "medicated atmosphere" like that of "wine during animated conversation." But Coleridge's subsequent line of thought, that "every passion has its proper pulse," is closer to the truth, with its implication that poetic rhythm does not necessarily serve a function but is present as a matter of propriety. Rhythm is part of a convention adapted, Coleridge seems to be arguing, for a limited, specialized range of subject matter, one involving "passion." The word "passion" returns us directly to the question of what it is that the convention of poetry is especially adapted to measure. Is it, as Coleridge shrewdly suggests, "every passion"? Perhaps it is, though I would prefer the word "value," a concept strongly implicit in the word "passion"; for what is "passion" if not the fervent valuation of competing alternatives in some dramatic context?

We know that poems often assume other tasks than that of valuation. They tell stories. They give instructions. They flourish wit. We know, also, that other genres handle many of these tasks better than poetry. Novels are, by virtue of their length, by virtue of all the conventions of prose fiction, the most convenient format in which to portray human character and the swerving inner lives of people under the stress of changing circumstances and conflicts, in a realistically rendered historical context. Short stories are the most efficient and convenient conventional structures in which to present, replete with dialogue and details of setting, significant vignettes from people's lives. Indeed, the evolved literary genres tend to define each other's potentialities, to correct and to guide one another. One should probably not, for example, interrupt a briskly moving story to dwell on subtle moods of weather, on hints of winter light on the edges of clouds, or on the nuances and textures of a word or a phrase. Such material probably better belongs in a poem. Preaching properly belongs in sermons or in self-help manuals. We know, too, that the poem, unlike the novel or drama, has always encouraged the foregrounding of issues involving valuation, detaching such issues from the kinds of full-fledged plots and detailed human predicaments that are common and conventional in prose fiction. Moreover, because the most fundamental element of poetic convention is its display, whether through prosody, through figurative language, or through both, of a conspicuously pleasing verbal surface, at least some of the material whose value a poem attempts to measure will be language itself. It will measure the values of its own language as it goes along.

How can language measure its own value without reference to some extrinsic, critical meta-language? Through prosody, which in poetry is roughly equivalent to what formal proof is in mathematics. To fully understand how this happens, let us consider more precisely the meaning of "measurement," a word which I have been using rather cavalierly up to this point. Mathematics, the science of number, evolved as a means of measuring the physical world and for orientation within it. After "number," probably the most fundamental mathematical concept is that of ratio. Units of measure are meaningful *only* in terms of ratio. That a home run traveled five hundred feet in the air or that a basketball center is seven feet two inches tall are facts that have meaning only in terms of our sense of what *one* foot means: that is, by comparison with some unit with which we are familiar. In other words, for a measurement, for a ratio, to alert us to its significance, it must refer to our expectations and to our remembered experiences, and it must play off of them. Of course, value which is not monetary—and particularly the value of things in themselves—cannot be framed in terms of number, and therefore it cannot, strictly speaking, be measured in terms of ratio. But if ratio is simply one form of comparison—a numerical comparison—and if, as I maintain, even in numerical comparisons ratio carries rhetorical weight only as it conspicuously accords with or violates our expectations, then we can see immediately how prosody can wring value from language itself and measure that value. To take but one example, consider how, in an accentual-syllabic prosody, the meter, because it affects every discrete syllable, foregrounds it:

> How sweet I roam'd from field to field,
>   And tasted all the summer's pride,
> 'Till I the prince of love beheld,
>   Who in the sunny beams did glide!

Each syllable, like a palpable nugget of paint laid on in *impasto*, assumes a value independent of the word in which it occurs; and by so conspicuously dividing language into units, the iambic tetrameter focuses unaccustomed attention on each unit. The "meta-language"—the denominator implicitly weighing the numerator of Blake's language here—consists of ordinary speech and written prose. We begin to linger over the syllables in the Blake poem, to relish them by comparison to "ordinary" syllables. Suddenly, through contrast, the value inherent in the poem's language is lifted into prominence; and this contrast, though nonnumerical, is equivalent to our apprehension of ratio.

Needless to say, the beauty of good poetic language can have its source in any number of different kinds of "ratio"—so many overlapping kinds that it would be futile and pedantic to try to list, codify, or methodize them. The point of the example above is only to suggest, by illustration, a general principle: that "value" in poetry is measured and expressed by "ratio," and that the greater the organization in a poem, the more prominently will such "ratios" be thrown into relief.

This same principle may hold, also, for a poem's subject matter, to the extent that "subject matter" can be considered as independent of a poem's language, as something which that language is trying to "express." Because, in good poems, structure (how "one element follows another," as Barbara Herrnstein Smith shrewdly puts it) is more highly organized over a shorter interval than in other modes of discourse, the values inherent in a poem's subject matter will, as I have suggested earlier, be thrown more prominently and more immediately into the foreground than in other modes. Value will tend to *be* the main subject matter of the poem. Indeed, it would seem to be virtually self-evident that the length of a discourse must profoundly influence how much emphasis over a given interval a given "ratio" will receive. The shorter a poem, the heavier the emphasis on any one word or sound or figure of speech. Conversely, good poems can *afford* to be shorter than, say, good short stories or novels, *because* of a poem's comparatively high density of local effects, because of the comparative frequency of the "ratios" which these effects project. And this, as I have already suggested, is one of the principal ways that genres tend to define one another and to circumscribe their own areas of maximum potentiality. Indeed, even Poe's seemingly arbitrary limit of one hundred effective lines for a poem, when viewed in this light, acquires a certain plausibility.

What I have proposed, somewhat playfully, as the "inexpressibility" theorem of poetry—the notion that the very raison d'être of a poem's specialized language, like that of mathematical language, is its ability to measure, to express subject matter which, without the conventions of this language, would elude us—should not, of course, be taken too strictly. Whereas a concept such as "acceleration" is untranslatable from mathematical language, most poems are at least partially translatable, more so, at least, than Stevens's "Sea Surface Full of Clouds," which I adduced only in order to demonstrate the full implications of the analogy between poetry and mathematics when it is carried out thoroughly. Most poetry, thank heavens, is far less "pure" than what Valéry envisioned or than Stevens's "Sea Surface Full of Clouds." Pope's notion of "true wit" as "What oft was thought, but ne'er so well expressed" does not, for example, acknowledge the issue of inexpressibility. He probably means, "What oft was *said*, but ne'er so well expressed." His formulation is a preromantic one. It does not acknowledge intuition. It forms a sort of lower limit for the subject matter of poetry. The range of most poetic subject matter may be located somewhere between this lower limit and Auden's "smiling secret" that we "cannot quote," the upper limit. Somewhere above this limit, presently out of bounds, might be located Mallarmé's "flower absent from all bouquets." Within these limits may be located subject matter such as we find in the following passage from Hopkins's "Binsey Poplars":

> My aspens dear, whose airy cages quelled,
> Quelled or quenched in leaves the leaping sun,
> Are felled, felled, are all felled;
>> Of a fresh and following folded rank
>>> Not spared, not one
>>> That dandled a sandalled
>> Shadow that swam or sank
> On meadow and river and wind-wandering weed-
>> winding bank.

In its context, the passage "That dandled a sandalled / Shadow that swam or sank / On meadow and river . . ." constitutes what I would guess will remain the single most sufficient description in English that we will ever have of the peculiarly arresting motion of aspen leaves and their shadows in a light breeze, of the way those shadows seem to tumble and flutter as if they were underwater, the way they seem to revolve without getting anywhere, of the way the sunlight on the ground around them waxes and wanes like the light wavering on the bottom of a flowing brook, of the joyous, animate, almost playful way in which the shadows and the leaves all seem to dance together, of the way they "dandle." But already the poem's terms are tempting us back to them, away from our clumsy approximations and provisional lists. Other languages can *approximate* the true essence of aspen-leaf movement, but they cannot measure it as precisely as this poem's language can; nor can they exactly translate this poem's language, which remains the single perfect formula not only for the inscape of those lost trees but for all the aspens that I can remember and—because poetic language as fully realized as Hopkins's bequeaths us formulas so powerful as to be nearly universal—the rest of the aspens I will ever see and sit under and relish redundantly.

9. Landscape Poems

Probably anybody who composes poetry regularly is familiar with the temptation to begin writing about what is immediately visible outside the window, to project one's own mood and preoccupations upon that landscape and thus to indulge the time-honored "pathetic fallacy." There are a variety of reasons for this impulse, all of them good. The first is that of simple availability. The landscape—the trees and the weather beyond the window—is present, impinging with its small or large consequences on our lives. A second temptation is almost corollary to the first. The dominion of landscape and weather is of such a scale that any poem about it has the instant potential for something approaching universality. Its images, its symbols, or, to borrow T. E. Hulme's handy generic term, its "counters," will be familiar to everybody. A poet of landscape has the enviable advantage of working in what amounts to a universal language. This universality of what might be called "landscape typology" suggests a third reason behind the poet's immediate impulse to landscape. Although most landscape poems tend to be conspicuously more psychological than other kinds of poems—as the very notion of the "pathetic fallacy" implies, landscapes will often function like inkblots—once completed, a landscape poem, perhaps because of its resemblance to a painting, will tend, like a work of visual art, to acquire some of the fine, hard impersonality of an object. Reading a good landscape poem, our attention is distracted away from what T. E. Hulme once called the poet's "moan" and toward the formal elements of the work itself. Indeed, the modernist movement in English language poetry may be seen, in large part, as an attempt to make poems which, like painting or sculpture, could exist independently of the squalid biography or the inner life of their author.

The poem of landscape, however, confronts the poet with difficulties just as great as are the apparent advantages of painterly impersonality. The first one is obvious. Paint is a far better medium for rendering nuances of light, color, and form than language is. A poet trying to describe autumn colors, "red, orange, yellow, crimson," simply cannot compete with even a mediocre painter. Compared with paint, the words describing visual phenomena remain hopelessly abstract. Paint, then, is the best medium for rendering special kinds of subject matter, just as extensive prose narration containing dialogue and internal monologue—those elements which make up that genre known as the novel—would seem to comprise the most efficient way of rendering the shape and drift of individual human character under the stress of worldly circumstances—a better way than cinema, which, because it cannot render the interior lives of people as fluently as literature can, is limited significantly to presenting human action in what must always remain a relatively documentary style. It is in ways like this that not only the various artistic media but also, within a given medium such as literature, the various "genres" define themselves and develop roughly with respect to one another as a system of mutually compensatory potentialities, or what a friend of mine once termed an "ecology." Poems of landscape compete implicitly with paintings; but in order for either the landscape painting or the landscape poem to offer a valid raison d'être, each must do things which the other cannot. Indeed, by this line of reasoning, we could extrapolate and predict virtually all of the principal elements in both.

What will the achieved poem of landscape present more effectively than any painting could? Action, a sense of the passage of time, a sense of process and of things not immediately, physically present or visible. What will the achieved realistic landscape painting present more effectively than a poem could? Visual accuracy, precise qualities of light (and shadow) as registered on the limned forms of trees, buildings, hills, on what is present and visible. Moreover, if the painting is any good, such qualities of light will be more subtle and palpable than can be captured in any photograph; for in a painting this subject matter—for example the complex interrelationships of color whereby every given color within a visual field defines every other color—will be interpreted and edited not as photography does but as the unmediated human eye and mind do.

Although it is the possibility of representing action in time which affords the landscape poem opportunities denied to the painter, it is the very painterly nature of the landscape poem which makes it so difficult to present such action; for in order that there be action, there must be an actor, a protagonist. The poem of landscape, however, as I have already suggested, is almost by definition focused *not* on a character but outward, on a landscape. How can the poet create action in a setting which would seem to be inherently static and without people? A paradigm of how the achieved poem of landscape negotiates such a paradoxical set of requirements may be seen in Emily Dickinson's "A Certain Slant of Light":

> There's a certain Slant of light,
> Winter Afternoons—
> That oppresses, like the Heft
> Of Cathedral Tunes—
>
> Heavenly Hurt, it gives us—
> We can find no scar,
> But internal difference,
> Where the Meanings, are—
>
> None may teach it—Any—
> 'Tis the Seal Despair—
> An imperial affliction
> Sent us of the Air—
>
> When it comes, the Landscape listens—
> Shadows—hold their breath—
> When it goes, 'tis like the Distance
> On the look of Death—

We might first note that, beautiful as the poem is, the satisfactions which it affords us are not primarily visual. Even though it is focused outward on a natural scene, it does not mention a single color or describe a single form. Are we looking at woods, a lawn, a grove, fields, hills? Is there snow on the ground? We are not sure. What is the weather? Is it a bleakly clear, hard, dry afternoon? Or does the sun break through the clouds in one brief, poignant slant? Is it early to mid afternoon, or later? Does the sunlight fade because of sunset or because of cloud cover? My guess—which is only intuitive and based upon my memories of growing up in northern New Jersey—is that it is not sunset, that the day is mostly cloudy, very forlorn, that around three in the afternoon the sun appears through a rift in the stratus, infinitely tantalizing, melancholy, like the reminder of some other life, some other season, some other realm (perhaps heavenly) than the claustral, futureless gray of winter. But this is pure guesswork, without a shred of textual backing.

Despite its visual vagueness, however, the poem does in many ways resemble a painting. Its attention is directed outward at a landscape, not at the author/speaker herself or some other human protagonist. It is true that the implied author constitutes a definite presence in this poem—a more pronounced presence than we feel a painter has in a typical landscape painting—but she never refers to herself as taking action. She does not walk to a window. She does not pour a cup of tea. She does not sigh or weep. She simply looks.

Where, then, is that action which distinguishes literature from painting and without which neither this nor any poem can successfully compete with a good painting? Obviously it is in the scene itself, and it is made possible by the fact that, although the poem has the feel of a painting, the duration over which it scans its landscape is longer than the instantaneous "duration" captured in a painting. Within this duration, "When it comes . . . When it goes," different events take place, events whose source is not human. Indeed, the protagonist of the poem *is* the landscape itself, whose "Slant of light" *does* things ("oppresses," "comes," "goes"), a landscape which "listens" and whose "Shadows—hold their breath." The poem, then, is, in addition to its other implications, very much about time. It presents, to borrow Wordsworth's expression, a "spot of time." True, good realistic landscape paintings can, in spite of the static nature of a painting, evoke the temporal. The great realistic paintings of Edward Hopper, in which the main source of light is usually rather low, casting fairly dramatic shadows, approach as closely as painting can the dramatization of temporal process. Hopper's famous storefront painting, "Early Sunday Morning," for example, although it never shows the sun or the eastern sky directly, is about the sunrise, depicting it through the effect of the rising sun's light on a building. The painting is highly dramatic. Every shadow is about to go places, is poised in midcourse. The light in the painting holds that poise, displays the same suspense which we find in the best Monet. In the Dickinson poem, on the other hand, we trace the entire process of the sun-slant's almost apparitional arrival though to its fading. The shadows reach their destinations.

*   *   *   *

Despite their different potentialities, landscape paintings and landscape poems have one important thing in common. They arise from the same aesthetic impulse. What is this impulse? One component of it is the conviction, on the part of the observer, that the type of experience found in the landscape is, as I have already suggested, "universal," that what I have referred to as the "typology" of accurately observed landscape is a typology about which there would be, if people were polled, a surprisingly strong consensus. How deeply this tacit assumption is embodied in the Dickinson poem is evident in its rhetorical stance; for there is a second main character in the Dickinson poem, a plural pronoun, "We . . . us," who bears much the same relation to the poem's landscape as a viewer does to a painting, and the style with which this pronoun presents its observations is profoundly revealing as to the kind of aesthetic "knowledge" which constitutes the impulse behind poems and paintings of landscape. We note, first, that this style is almost brazenly assertive, as if the speaker were absolutely certain that her description of what might at first be regarded as a private, wholly subjective vision were (1) common to us all; (2) familiar and repeatable; (3) based not upon the observer's mood but upon objective facts "out there" in the landscape. The poem says, in effect, "I am going to describe a certain type of emotional and spiritual experience which winter light on a landscape produced in me, and I am going to do this so accurately that you will immediately recognize that this type of landscape evokes in you an identical response." Hence the plural pronoun, the confident, declarative tone, the plural "afternoons" suggesting the typical nature of this "Slant of light," and our overall feeling that the landscape is not being transformed into allegory but is simply being described. Such claims are large ones, but they have some plausibility. To see how this might be so, let us examine a second poem which, though not en-

tirely devoted to landscape, is strikingly reminiscent of the
Dickinson poem and is perhaps conscious of this, William
Stafford's "Long Distance":

> Sometimes when you watch the fire
> ashes glow and gray
> the way the sun turned cold on spires
> in winter in the town back home
> so far away.
>
> Sometimes on the telephone
> the one you hear goes far
> and ghostly voices whisper in.
> You think they are from other wires.
> You think they are.

Here, as in the Dickinson poem, a certain winter light takes
on a sinister beauty, becomes a faint, ethereal portent of the
beholder's profound intimation not only of mortality but also
of his absolute aloneness as an organism. The power of this
poem stems largely from its accuracy of observation; but the
power is also rhetorical. Like Dickinson's poem, this one advances a description of what might at first be regarded as a
private, wholly subjective experience as if that experience
were both common and repeatable. The poem's "you" is the
equivalent of Dickinson's "We," and the word "Sometimes"
has the same degree of confident assertiveness as Dickinson's
plural "afternoons." As with the Dickinson poem, we feel the
speaker's sense of recognition of something in the landscape,
a kindredness across great distance, epitomized in the second
stanza, which compares the winter light to the memory of the
once-familiar voices of people who have died. Like the Dickinson poem, this one ends on a note of profound loneliness
amidst desolation. Following the call outward toward the
winter light, the speaker, who cannot join the light and the
utter otherness of the landscape, is left stranded.

Stafford's poem "Things We Did That Meant Something" describes the same type of recognition, but with a slightly different emphasis:

> Thin as memory to a bloodhound's nose,
> being the edge of some new knowing,
> I often glance at a winter color—
> husk or stalk, a sunlight touch,

maybe a wasp nest in the brush
near the winter river with silt like silver.

Once with a slingshot I hit a wasp nest:—
without direction but sure of right,
released from belief and into act,
hornets planed off by their sincere faith.
Vehement response for them was enough,
patrolling my head with its thought like a moth:—

"Sometime the world may be hit like this
or I getting lost may walk toward this color
far in old sunlight with no trace at all,
till only the grass will know I fall."

Of particular interest in this poem is the word "memory" in
conjunction with the word "new." The poem is explicitly
about the paradoxical nature of déjà vu. A flash of memory—
of something old and past—Stafford characterizes as "new
knowledge." It is this type of déjà vu, what Wordsworth
called a "visionary gleam," that constitutes the impulse that
lies both behind realistic poems of landscape and behind
most realistic landscape paintings. The artist is struck by intimations of some elusive knowledge inherent in the landscape itself.

Sometimes such knowledge cannot be wholly imparted.
Stafford's poem "Across Kansas," for example, is clearly about
déjà vu, about the overwhelming wonderment at returning to
a remembered landscape and finding new knowledge in
"every rock":

My family slept those level miles
but like a bell rung deep till dawn
I drove down an aisle of sound,
nothing real but in the bell,
past the town where I was born.

Once you cross a land like that
you own your face more: what the light
struck told a self; every rock
denied all the rest of the world.
We stopped at Sharon Springs and ate—

My state still dark, my dream too long to tell.

This poem is exceedingly clever in the way that it marshals a
gorgeous density of sound. It not only resonates and rings

like a bell, but its content is epitomized in the pun "told a self," so that throughout the remainder of the poem the verbs "to toll" and "to tell" are interchangeable. Nevertheless, the experience which the poem describes remains almost wholly subjective, restricted, perhaps, to "My family." Indeed, as the singular first-person pronouns and the poem's final admission, "my dream too long to tell," indicate, the poet recognizes that his experience may in this case be largely incommunicable.

*   *   *   *

The comparative failure of "Across Kansas" to transcend the subjectivity of its vision suggests a great deal about the strengths and limitations of landscape poems. Although, as I have already suggested, the impulse behind landscape poems is connected to feelings of déjà vu—to convictions of profound yet seemingly unaccountable familiarity—if we compare "Across Kansas" with the Dickinson poem or with the first two Stafford poems, we see that they deal not only with different degrees of familiarity but with different kinds as well. The Dickinson poem, like the first two Stafford poems, depicts for us a startlingly familiar slant of light, but in a generic landscape. These poems are oriented far more with respect to time than to place; they are addressed to a community of people; and they have a religious quality to their vision. "Across Kansas," however, as the very presence of a place name in its title would indicate, is about the seemingly ineffable genius of a particular place. It is more lyric in quality, in that the "I" is musing largely to himself. Its vision tends to be more psychological than religious.

As "Across Kansas" indicates, when landscape poems attempt to capture the intimacy of a particular place, to carry over into the public domain of literature what Hopkins so tellingly referred to as "inscape," the poet's task is far harder than that of rendering a "spot of time." For the dialect of any given "place," especially of "home," exists not only in a severely limited domain, but the details which compose it are far more idiosyncratic and of more deeply private significance than the elements which make up the grand typology of weather and season. We could probably arrive at something like a consensus about the luminous excitement one feels at waking up to the first snowfall of the year, wherever it happened. A far more difficult task is set, however, when we try to communicate to a public the peculiarly solicitous way in which the head of a tree outside one's bedroom window might seem to preside over one's childhood bedroom; or the way in which that or any familiar piece of local landscape may seem, at times, almost to recognize you, the beholder. Some kinds of landscapes, of course, by their very nature seem to recognize the beholder, to gesture a greeting. The spectacular sandstone formations of the Southwest, for example, often seem literally to gesture at us, to incorporate something tantamount to facial expressions, as if the land were speaking to us in an exotic dialect, one just about to break into sense. In response, we start naming the rocks, as though by naming them we could possess them—the Three Judges, Table Rock, and what not. Such landscapes affect us in much the same way that officially beautiful women affect men. Because a beauty queen's beauty is so wholly without individuality—is a composite of publicly acclaimed features— it seems somehow automatically available. It seems to establish intimacy with everybody at once. We feel as though it had always been "ours"; such landscapes function like inkblots, absorbing the full library of an individual's fantasies. This is why, I think, in landscapes which display obviously evocative features, the names which the eroded rocks end up with are so blandly mimetic and cartoonish. Table Rock, Mirror Lake, Cathedral Rock: the aesthetic experience of place is so private that such blunt, public names are the only ones which people can agree upon. Hence, although the experience of returning "home," of witnessing a face or a landscape which wears the unique and ineffably familiar expression of a loved one or a relative, is perhaps the most consistently powerful aesthetic experience most of us have, it also remains largely incommunicable. But not, perhaps, entirely. Consider for example the following poem by the poet who was and who will probably always remain America's most accomplished poet of landscape, Richard Hugo:

West Marginal Way

One tug pounds to haul an afternoon
of logs up river. The shade
of Pigeon Hill across the bulges
in the concrete crawls on reeds
in a short field, cools a pier
and the violence of young men
after cod. The crackpot chapel
with a sign erased by rain, returned
before to calm and a mossed roof.

A dim wind blows the roses
growing where they please. Lawns
are wild and lots are undefined
as if the payment made in cash
were counted then and there.

These names on boxes will return
with salmon money in the fall,
come drunk down the cinder arrow
of a trail, past the store of Popich,
sawdust piles and the saw mill
bombing air with optimistic sparks,
blinding gravel pits and the brickyard
baking, to wives who taught themselves
the casual thirst of many summers
wet in heat and taken by the sea.

Some places are forever afternoon.
Across the road and a short field
there is the river, split and yellow
and this far down affected by the tide.

This poem, Hugo's earliest published poem but still one of his best, takes on the nearly impossible task of trying to capture the peculiar genius of a place for a public which has never been there, to render precisely its unique mood, as if this scene were, to borrow Hugo's private aesthetic terminology, his personal "home." True, the poem can—and perhaps it should—be read first not as a landscape poem but as an allegory for the moody, stagnant state of Hugo's inner life when he was in his early twenties and living with his grandparents. But it also, I think, brings into subtle relief the unique character of a place and makes such seemingly subjective and incommunicable knowledge at least partially available to us; and it does so, not surprisingly, in that sweeping and assertive rhetoric which characterizes, we have seen, so many landscape poems. "Some places are forever afternoon," the poem's best line as well as its most assertive, presents the genius of place in temporal and hence in nearly universal terms. But the rest of the poem establishes intimacy of place differently, in an unprecedented manner which Hugo had to invent single-handedly. Every element singled out for notice in this landscape has its own story, its own little legend which defines that element's uniqueness, its character. The "pier," regularly "cooled" by afternoon shade, is the regular site of "violence of young men / after cod." The chapel's history is somehow "crackpot" and it has "returned / . . . to calm." The "Lawns" and "lots" have a marginal, unkempt air defined by the human history of the place, "as if the payment made in cash / were counted then and there." In short, much, though not all, of the unique feel of the place is presented as a sort of speculative but plausible gossip about its human and inhuman inhabitants, whose histories and whose behavior are imprinted in the very scene itself. To borrow the implicit metaphor of "home" which lies always at the heart of Hugo's poetry: it is as if the elements, human and inhuman, which made up this scene were all members of one extended family, in which everybody knew the biography of everybody else. In this sense, the place does indeed resemble "home," a place where the private history of everything is mutually known, where everybody and everything is, in a sense, one's relative.

The final stanza describes beautifully the oddly isolated, somewhat claustral feel of the place. "And this far down affected by the tide" renders very accurately the sense of something grander, more liberating, yet perhaps menacing—the sea—rumored to exist beyond the precincts of this odd, backward "family" with its "names on boxes," its resolute but unprogressive sawmill, its "wives" who endure the place "wet in heat," its routine afternoon drama of a pounding tug arriving, as if on schedule, like the mail. If, as the Dickinson poem would suggest, the genius of a landscape glimpsed with respect to time is best rendered through the typology of weather and of season, the Hugo poem would suggest that the genius of landscape with respect to space—as "place"—is best rendered through its history, through the accumulation of civilized action and gossip that has already given every person and thing its identity, its name. Want of just this type of gossip, of such stories, is what leaves "Across Kansas" only partially realized.

*   *   *   *

It is story which gives "West Marginal Way" its drama. It is story—the behavior of the protagonist, Light—which gives the Dickinson poem its drama; and it is instructive, I think, to note the different way in which the drama "works"—that is, creates suspense—in each of these poems. In the Dickinson poem, the suspense arises from the poignancy and desperation of the author/speaker's trying to possess a moment which is elusive. In the Hugo poem, on the other hand, the drama arises from the opposite predicament. There is the potentiality of action, of change, of release—the elements of the landscape have their histories, and the sea lies alluringly like a glamorous rumor over the horizon—but nothing is getting anywhere. The tug is stuck on its monotonous afternoon schedule. The tide is on schedule, while the buildings and humans are all quietly rotting together "at home." The suspense of this poem arises from our subliminal but quite pronounced sense of action which, though potential, remains *unaccomplished*. We wonder: When is something going to break? How long can this situation last? The poem leaves us sad and uneasy. There is too much fury pent up in this "home."

Action and story have, of course, always been ingredients as essential to poems as to prose fiction. The Stafford, the Dickinson, and the Hugo poems all illustrate how elimination of an active human protagonist as the foreground for a poem immediately and drastically increases the difficulty of poetic composition by denying the poet the main potentialities of his genre, indeed, of his medium. In the Dickinson and Hugo poems in particular, we watch the poet having tackled a painterly subject trying to smuggle elements of story, of action, back into the scene. These poems, by using the static medium of painting as an implicit analogue for a poem, demonstrate the limits of poetry as a genre. It must present action or it will lose its principal aesthetic advantage. But if, in poems of landscape, the poet resists the temptation to be painterly, his task seems to become much easier. In the poetry of Words-

worth, for example—and he is still, to my mind, our greatest "landscape" poet in English—we see that although his
regard for landscape arises out of the very impulses lying
behind both landscape painting and poems of landscape—
from profound intimations of familiarity and kindredness
with parts of the physical world—his poems seem to recognize that the inherent strengths of literature arise from
story and action, from temporal rather than spatial modes of
perception and organization, even though a landscape may
momentarily seduce us with the dream of stasis and hold us
entranced with something like a human expression on its
countenance. Reading Wordsworth, I am always reminded of
the psycholinguistic theories of Jacques Lacan—his notion
that because we acquire language at the same time as we are
learning that our being is indeed separate from that of our
mothers, that because words are insufficient substitutes for
immediate maternal gratification, language is inherently filled
with pre-Oedipal grief, that, in the words of Robert Hass's
now famous "Meditation at Lagunitas," "a word is elegy to
what it signifies."

In Lacanian terms, much of Wordsworth might be regarded
as a hopeful, elegaic attempt by the poet to chant back the
numinous, enfolding presence of his mother, to recover what
Lacanians call the "mirror stage," before she was distanced
and incarnated in the abstraction "Nature." Indeed, I think
that it is probably no accident that so many landscape poems
implicitly, or, as in the case of Wordsworth, explicitly, repre-
sent landscape as feminine and maternal. But if we compare
any of the famous "spots of time" in Wordsworth's *Prelude*
with the Dickinson poem or with "West Marginal Way," we
see that, although the type of experience which Wordsworth
has with his landscapes—"Gleams like the flashings of a
shield;—the earth / And common face of Nature spake to me /
Rememberable things"—is similar to the kind of experience
which Hugo and Dickinson describe, in that it consists of intuitive flashes of recognition and remembered familiarity,
there is one great difference between them that is at least as
significant as this similarity. Whereas there is a heavy list-
lessness—an expectant but deathly passivity—in the Dickinson and the Hugo, as if the poet longed subliminally to re-
gress, to lose self-consciousness and differentiation, in *The
Prelude* the speaker is much more emphatically foregrounded

and engaged in much more activity. In virtually all of the "spots of time" in which landscape figures prominently, the protagonist remains not the landscape but the speaker himself. Compared to the Hugo or the Dickinson personae, he is *very* aggressive, hiking, skating, rowing, stealing birds' eggs. Consider, for example, the famous stolen-boat episode in Book I:

> One summer evening (led by her) I found
> A little boat tied to a willow tree
> Within a rocky cave, its usual home.
> Straight I unloosed her chain, and stepping in
> Pushed from the shore. It was an act of stealth
> And troubled pleasure, nor without the voice
> Of mountain-echoes did my boat move on;
> Leaving behind her still, on either side,
> Small circles glittering idly in the moon,
>
> . . . .
>
> With an unswerving line, I fixed my view
> Upon the summit of a craggy ridge,
> The horizon's utmost boundary; for above
> Was nothing but the stars and the grey sky.
> She was an elfin pinnace; lustily
> I dipped my oars into the silent lake,
> And, as I rose upon the stroke, my boat
> Went heaving through the water like a swan;
> When, from behind that craggy steep till then
> The horizon's bound, a huge peak, black and huge,
> As if with voluntary power instinct
> Upreared its head. I struck and struck again,
> And growing still in stature the grim shape
> Towered up between me and the stars, and still,
> For so it seemed, with purpose of its own
> And measured motion like a living thing,
> Strode after me. . . .

Although this passage starts out with a disclaimer that the poet was "led by her," added as a parenthetical afterthought, our sense of this passage is that the chief agent of this episode is the poet himself; for without his action, as a simple diagram of the geography of the scene will remind us, there could be no reciprocal action in the landscape. For this reason, I would suggest that, in psychological terms, Wordsworth's landscapes are much further advanced than those of Dickinson and Hugo. They reflect the vision of a writer who has passed beyond a paralyzed, pining, "oral" stage of development and into a "phallic" stage.[1] And, indeed, even the biographies of these poets would support this difference. In Hugo's "West Marginal Way," for example, language seems to function much as Lacan suggests. It serves as a diluted, insufficient substitute for the poet's vaguely intimated, original merger of his identity with some nurturing Other. From this poem alone, any analyst could guess that the rest of Hugo's poetry would be equally "Lacanian," revealing a conspicuously arrested development in aspects of the poet's personality, and that this poem sprang out of radical need. In fact, most of Hugo's poems, with their central metaphor of "home," do attempt, over and over again, obsessively, to realize the same project as "West Marginal Way," that of making the poet imaginatively at "home" in a landscape—by means of mere words to imbue each landscape with a comforting intimacy which Hugo himself, in his semi-orphaned childhood, had never enjoyed.

If we turn to the Wordsworth passage, on the other hand, we see that a strict Lacanian interpretation does not comfortably apply to Wordsworth. Whereas in the Hugo poem we see language used in a compensatory way, to fill an endless absence, while the poet himself remains immobilized by grief and need, in the Wordsworth passage the poet's vision of the lost, feminine world of nature is triggered first by action and only secondarily by language. Thus Lacan's belief that *all* language is inherently, to borrow Hass's term, "elegy," accurately describes the Hugo poem but not the Wordsworth. Although the Wordsworth passage implicitly laments some original separation between poet and mother (incarnated in Nature), it does not, like Hugo's "West Marginal Way," attempt to substitute language for absence. To be sure, we could draw an analogy between *The Prelude* and Wordsworth's fall from childhood, on the one hand, and language and our fall from

1. Although the Wordsworth passage contains some "phallic" imagery, including the sonic resemblance of "pinnace" (a light sailing vessel) to "penis," I find it unfortunate that, because of Freud, adult initiative, male *or* female, should have come to be identified with the phallus. But this appears to be the terminology—the psychological jargon—that we are still stuck with. I use it here only for convenience, as a sort of shorthand—an inadequate one—for some better term which, if it has been invented, has not yet achieved full currency.

some pre-Oedipal "mirror stage," on the other. But to conclude from this or from any particular poem that *all* language is "elegy" is to make an intellectually provocative but serious blur in the distinction between analogy and identity.

This distinction between analogy and identity applies significantly to the similarities and differences between poems and paintings, and it suggests that confusions of media—the desire of a poet to make a very painterly poem—may arise out of the deepest need, out of the writer's regressive attraction to the comforting stasis of the visual arts. Both the Hugo poem and the Dickinson poem subliminally long not just to be *like* a painting but to *be* a painting. They express a hatred of time and a desire for repose, a desire so strong that, in each case, it drove the writer against his or her own art. They virtually eliminate a human protagonist. The resulting responses to landscape emerge as tortured expressions of psychological frustration, "spots of time" in which time is incompletely apprehended, leaving the poet unredeemed, stranded in a static, visual "spot." In the Wordsworth passage, on the other hand, the figure of the poet is not paralyzed, not choked with the backlogged grief of some latent psychological crisis. He is free to move about in the foreground of his own experience, unafraid of time, absolved by the landscape and by his vision of it—a vision which, in its fullest development, is not static but dynamic, not psychological but religious. As Wordsworth wrote, immortally:

> There are in our existence spots of time,
> That with distinct pre-eminence retain
> A renovating virtue, whence, depressed
> By false opinion and contentious thought,
> Or aught of heavier or more deadly weight,
> In trivial occupations, and the round
> Of ordinary intercourse, our minds
> Are nourished and invisibly repaired;
> A virtue, by which pleasure is enhanced,
> That penetrates, enables us to mount,
> When high, more high, and lifts us up when fallen.

10. Poems versus Jokes

Are certain subjects inherently more suitable than other subjects are for poetry? It is, I think, a tacit and rather complacent assumption shared by poets today that with the advent of "modernism," as poetry freed itself from threadbare Victorian poetic diction and decorum, it was able to avail itself of an unlimited range of subject matter. Certainly the range broadened. In American poetry especially, beginning with Whitman, who was able to say in a poem, "The scent of my armpits aroma finer than prayer," we find a tradition inviting the poet to assimilate into poems an increasingly diverse assortment of experiences. Louis Simpson is very much aware of this legacy when he remarks in his famous poem "American Poetry" that "Whatever it is, it must have / A stomach that can digest / Rubber, coal, uranium, moons, poems." But there is a significant difference between the notion that a poem "must" be able to *digest . . .* Rubber" and the notion that a poem must be able to be *about* rubber, between a poem that mentions in passing the "armpits aroma" and a poem devoted entirely to armpits. Consider, for example, the following poemlike piece which a student submitted and read aloud to my poetry workshop, a "poem" with the unpromising title "Zits":

> In front of a mirror
> examining
> stuffed pores,
> red finger prints on
> white skin.
> A rag
> to rub away
> seven layers of skin
> after every meal.
> The overnight miracles
> of Clearasil, Stridex and
> Benzoil Peroxide

(Oxy 5, for short).
All in an effort
to prevent
not forest fires,
but something far more
disastrous—
a zit.
Let's see Smokey
stop one of these
with his shovel.

Both the form of the piece and the reaction of the class—
explosive laughter when he read it—suggest some of the limitations of subject matter in poetry, as well as the reasons for
such limitations. First, the verbal strategy of the student
"poem" is really that of a joke rather than a poem. Second,
joke-telling is an oral art that requires the complicity of a live
audience. By reading this "poem" aloud before a class, the
student duplicated these conditions. Indeed, the poem's subject matter, "zits," is more suitable to that convention—to that
"genre"—which we call The Joke than to that genre which we
call The Poem; and the reasons for this help to define not only
the kinds of limitations of subject matter appropriate to poetry but the nature of poetry itself.

Whereas poems are designed primarily as literature and
only secondarily for live performance, jokes are an exclusively
oral art form. As Freud put it:

Generally speaking, a . . . joke calls for three people: in addition to
the one who makes the joke, there must be a second who is taken as
the object of the hostile or sexual aggressiveness, and a third in
whom the joke's aim of producing pleasure is fulfilled.[1]

A broader, post-Freudian description of the joke's depen-
dence on live audience is given by G. Legman:

Under the mask of humor, our society allows infinite aggressions
by everyone and against everyone. In the culminating laugh by
the listener or observer—whose position is often really that of vic-
tim or butt—the teller of the joke betrays his hidden hostility and
signals his victory by being, theoretically at least, the one person
who does not laugh. . . . The listener's expected laughter is, there-

---

1. James Strachey, trans., *Jokes and Their Relation to the Unconscious* (New
York: Norton, 1960), pp. 100–101.

fore, . . . a shriving of the teller, a reassurance that he has not been caught . . . .[2]

As both Legman and Freud suggest, however, jokes, like poetry, are designed to deal with feeling. Whereas Freud calls this feeling "instinct (whether lustful or hostile)" of which the joke can "make possible the satisfaction . . . in the face of an obstacle," Legman suggests that the "retailing of obscenities" can have another purpose: "to absorb and control, even to slough off by means of . . . laughter, the great anxiety that both teller and listener feel in connection with certain culturally determined themes . . . venereal disease, homosexuality, and castration."

Jokes, then, treat of a limited range of feelings such as lust, hostility, and anxiety, and it is the nature of these feelings— they are mainly negative in the sense that they are not feelings which we voluntarily *choose*—which determines the elements that comprise the convention of the joke. How does this convention differ from that of a poem? In the joke-contract—the implicit set of expectations shared by the joke-teller and his (or her) listeners—both parties know in advance that the subject matter of the joke will be taboo, in the sense that the feelings which the joke treats would be, if expressed directly in public instead of through the joke-work, embarrassing to everybody present. Poems, on the other hand, do not set out explicitly, in the mind of either the poet or the reader, to deal with feelings which, because they are known in advance to be embarrassing, would invite concealment. Although some poems, for example Dickinson's "Wild Nights," may conceal erotic feelings, we do not sense when reading that poem that its author *intended* us to pick up any sexual double entendre or even to snicker. We do not sense that a coy method of concealment was ever part of a contract entered into by poet or reader.

Nevertheless, because both poems and jokes treat of feelings, both rely on similar-enough verbal strategies that it is no wonder, particularly in an oral setting—the setting so fundamental to the dynamic of The Joke—that a poem may function like a joke; for both rely on metaphorical indirection, traditionally the most efficient technique by which we render our

2. G. Legman, *Rationale of the Dirty Joke* (New York: Grove Press, 1968), p. 9.

feelings in language. As Freud puts it in his analysis of "smut," the verbal technique of the joke involves a process of "condensation accompanied by the formation of a substitute."[3] To observe this process at work in a joke, consider the following example of "smut": A man in the midst of intercourse with a voracious woman who is imploring him to go "further in" falls all the way "in" himself, tumbles through darkness, and finally lands on a spongy ground. He picks himself up, tries to find his bearings, but his new environment is pitch dark. Finally he sees a flashlight bobbing toward him faintly. The light turns out to belong to a second man. First man to newcomer: "Wh-where are we?" Answer: "I dunno, but if you'll help me find my car keys we can drive the hell out of here."

Here the formation of a substitute may be seen at two levels: (1) the entire joke may be regarded as a substitute—a metaphor—for a complex of feelings, in this case the anxiety which men may feel when confronted with a sexually voracious woman, a sense of inadequacy coupled with a fear of being swallowed whole; (2) within the joke, various elements have obvious symbolic value: the car, for example, symbolizes the autonomy and sense of phallic initiative which the threatened men want back. Similarly, in this joke, "condensation" may be regarded at two levels: (1) the entire joke may be taken as a "condensation" into one incident of male anxieties stemming from countless individual sexual exploits; (2) the contrary and complex feelings which the joke treats of are all synthesized and condensed into a punch line. Here, however, the similarities between this joke and a poem end. Whereas a poem attempts to clarify, to heighten, to reveal a valuable emotional truth, this joke attempts to disguise, to play down, to conceal an emotional truth which, though perhaps inevitable, is without value not only because it is unpleasant but because, like guilt, hatred, shame, fear, and self-disgust, it is debilitating, useless, ugly to behold both in others and in oneself. For this reason, the narrative, instead of sharpening these feelings, deliberately deadens them. It dehumanizes the female. She is merely a subhuman abyss that requires filling. Whereas in most poetry, the general is implied by the particular, here the particular is implied by the

3. Strachey, *Jokes*, p. 88.

general. The landscape and the protagonists are entirely hypothetical and generic, and the story's grotesque degree of exaggeration guarantees that the story is only hypothetical, not to be taken seriously. Similarly, the tone of the joke disguises feeling. It is only when covered by a tone of bluff, adolescent bravado—"We can drive the hell out of here"—that the fear of immolation and loss of male autonomy can be aired at all, by one male in the company of others.

In sum, then, jokes summon nasty feelings only in order to gain relief from them—to dispel them as efficiently as possible, either by gratifying them (the aggressive joke) or by ventilating them (the shameful joke), converting aggression and anxiety into the harmless and what Bergson has called the "anaesthetic" physiological response that we call laughter. It is this "anaesthetic" result of feeling converted to laughter that Freud is getting at when he writes that the pleasure we derive from jokes "arises from an economy in psychical expenditure"[4] and that in the use of jokes, the "yield of pleasure corresponds to the psychical expenditure that is saved."[5]

Poems, on the other hand, summon desirable feelings not in order to devalue them or to dispel them but in order to dwell on them, to work them up, to glorify them. Nevertheless, because poems tend, like jokes, to display "condensation" and "formation of a substitute," when poems are being read aloud by their authors, the social dynamic of the reading resembles a joke-telling session enough that an author may be tempted to use the reading as a joke-teller might—to slyly "confess," to express taboo feelings under the guise of art. If we picture the poem "Zits" being read before a live audience, we see that all four of the conditions necessary for a joke are met: (1) an oral setting; (2) an embarrassing subject; (3) verbal condensation and substitution; (4) jokelike cues assuring the audience that the speaker is *conscious* of the embarrassing nature of his subject matter. The poem-as-joke is both aggressive and cathartic. Smokey the Bear is the incarnation of a bland, forest-ranger, adult mentality that takes it for granted that one should stamp out pimples as readily as forest fires, when in fact earlier portions of the poem evince some covert fondness for "zits," while the final Smokey-the-

4. Ibid., p. 127.
5. Ibid., p. 118.

Bear reference contains a ring of defiance, a sneer at the rote values of official, adult life.

For the same reasons which turn the student poem into a joke, poems about sexuality, when they are read by their author before a live audience, may take on a jokelike character. If women are present and the reader is male, the poem may function just as Freud asserts that "smut" does—as a verbal rape. All of Richard Brautigan's erotic pieces are on the borderline between poems and jokes. Uttered before a live audience, they lose their character of being meditations on the taste of love; they become, instead, thinly veiled boasts, verbal seductions. Consider, for example, "Discovery":

> The petals of the vagina unfold
> like Christopher Columbus
> taking off his shoes.
>
> Is there anything more beautiful
> than the bow of a ship
> touching a new world?

The verbal structure of this poem, like that of a joke, employs substitution and condensation and builds to a sort of punch line. Indeed, so jokelike is this poem that whether we take it as a poem or as a joke depends entirely on the context in which we receive it. When we read it on the page, we take it as a poem, as a slight but accurate rendering of the lubricious anticipation a man might feel as he takes off his shoes on the way to the love bed. But read aloud the poem is merely a boast, an invitation. It ceases to be a poem for the same reason that, as Paul Valéry has written, "walking is like prose": instead of serving primarily as an end in itself, its verbal technique becomes merely a means to an end.

To see how this is so, let us compare the Brautigan poem with a passage of erotic poetry that is *not* jokelike in character: the last section of Roethke's beautiful "Words for the Wind":

> The breath of a long root,
> The shy perimeter
> Of the unfolding rose,
> The green, the altered leaf,
> The oyster's weeping foot,
> And the incipient star—

Are part of what she is.
She wakes the ends of life.

Being myself, I sing
The soul's immediate joy.
Light, light, where's my repose?
A wind wreathes round a tree.
A thing is done: a thing
Body and spirit know
When I do what she does:
Creaturely creature, she!

I kiss her moving mouth,
Her swart hilarious skin;
She breaks my breath in half;
She frolicks like a beast;
And I dance round and round,
A fond and foolish man,
And see and suffer myself
In another being, at last.

Whereas the Brautigan poem, read before a live audience, would provoke some snickering, the Roethke would not. Why not? Because the "immediate joy" which it celebrates is not a means to an end but an end in itself. The poem is suffused with a spirit of humility and awe before beauty. It evinces not the least taint of shame or even of lust, nor does it display any trace of deliberate concealment. So lyric is the Roethke—the speaker is singing to himself as if nobody else were present—that it makes absolutely no appeal to the audience, live or otherwise, to enlist it in a jokelike contract. What the speaker feels is "joy," an almost religious ecstasy, full of respect for the beloved, along with that subtle yet profound reassurance located at the very heart of sexual completion that he has been reconnected to "rose," "leaf," "oyster," and "star," to the world's body. Such feelings are more than physical. They are valuable in and of themselves. The Roethke passage could never be construed as merely a metaphor for satisfied sexual hunger.

The Brautigan "poem," on the other hand, is intended as a means to an end—to sexually arouse parts of the audience—and therefore it features pornographic detail, the word "vagina" and the coy closing image of "the bow of a ship / touching a new world," an image which, instead of evoking feeling, slyly suggests some of the mechanical details of coitus. Although this image, read on the page by a solitary reader, may, despite its smirking tone, evoke the wonder and strangeness of finding oneself "in another being, at last," its conspiratorial, ever so *knowing* tone, flaunted in front of a group, takes on an entirely different character: it becomes a dirty wink, a come-on.

The Valérian notion, then, that in poetry language is used as an end in itself whereas prose uses language as a means to an end suggests not only the fundamental difference between poems and jokes but also why certain subjects are more suitable for poems than for jokes, and why other subjects are more suitable for jokes than for poems. In a poem, nontaboo feelings are treated by language as having intrinsic value, as ends in themselves. In a joke, on the other hand, taboo feelings—feelings which are *de*valued—are summoned as means to an end: aggression or, as in the car-keys joke, relief from the feeling itself. Thus poems which deal with nasty subject matter—with material more suitable for jokes—imply more than an intellectual confusion of genre. They imply a devaluation of experience on the part of the author. Those who endorse the fashionable assumption that valid poems can be written about "anything" are, in effect, saying that they value all parts of their experience equally: the vista of a river, the stench of a latrine. That we find published poems about nasty subjects, even in good journals, does not imply vulgarity; it implies our general lack of confidence in what is valuable. Consider, for example, the following poem by Lyn Lifshin, originally published in *Poetry Now*:

1966 Healy

that we bought be
cause he couldn't
get it up made
him feel more a
man nearly we got
it when I sulked
and wouldn't go to
the chinese physics
teacher party
dressed as what
we dreamed we were
In boston people

        stopped to see their
        faces in the green
        glow but things
        started breaking
        right away and
        the green rusted

This poem is ugly because it does not, as beautiful art does, with subtlety and clarity discriminate between and measure the relative values in an experience or in the feelings attendant on that experience. Instead, the poem celebrates its speaker's sullenness, her very considerable skill at being snide. Everything the poem says reflects badly on the speaker—on her poor taste in boyfriends, on her inability to deal with a relationship, on her lack of compassion for her partner, on her crude, oversimplified interpretation of his behavior, on her evident contempt for "boston," on her tendency to dehumanize and write off people in general, physicists, Bostonians, Chinese, males. Like the Brautigan "poem," like smut, like my student's "poem" on "Zits," like all jokes, the Lifshin "poem" works only once—on the first reading. Once we "get it" and have laughed or snickered or winced, the energy charge of its feeling has been efficiently *dis*charged: *she* has relieved herself of cold fury; *we* have experienced a brief, dubious thrill of satisfaction, watching a target be hit. None of the feelings which the poem deals with is worth dwelling on or going back to. It is merely a joke masquerading as art, and a bad, ill-tempered joke at that.

No joke can be beautiful, like the Roethke poem; for jokes are not intended to be beautiful. Because the kinds of feeling which they treat of lack intrinsic value, instead of clarifying and intensifying feeling—valuing it for its own sake—jokes obscure feeling in order to exploit it as a means to an end or to dismiss it, converting their material not into the aesthetic response of wonder but into unfeeling, unbeauty—the unaesthetic spasms of laughter.

11. Style, Authenticity, and Poetic Truth

In the Winter 1981 *Georgia Review*, responding to an essay by Christopher Clausen, "Poetry in a Discouraging Time," which argued that "the rise of science has had something to do with displacing [poetry] as a publicly important vehicle for those truths that people accept as being centrally important," Hayden Carruth suggests that it is advertising, not "science," which is the true enemy of poetry. Carruth points to

> . . . the observable and growing distrust of language in general. It began long before the advent of electronic transmission, . . . I mean the iniquity of the first publican who hung out a sign saying that his beer was "better" when his clients, relying on their senses, could tell immediately that it was awful. The iniquity has been augmented to utterly horrifying dimensions in our time. . . . Children today are taught, in lessons compounded every five minutes, that untruth may be uttered with impunity, even with approval. Lying has become a way of life, very nearly now *the* way of life, in our society. The average adult American of average intelligence and average education believes almost nothing communicated to him in language, and the disbelief has become so ingrained that he or she does not even notice it. In short, the advertising business. . . . Advertising is the most corrupt and corrupting mental activity of the human race. It has invaded and destroyed every sector of language. . . . It has not only destroyed language, it has directly caused the increase of violence in our civil life, of death and misery, of war.

In this eloquent statement, Carruth suggests just why the particular nature of what the philosopher Philip Wheelwright has called "poetic truth"—why good poetry itself—is as necessary to us today as it ever has been, perhaps more so, is necessary to us both individually and collectively.

What is "poetic truth"? It is tempting to recite a great poem such as Frost's "After Apple-Picking" and then say simply, "There now." Great poems, as we know, tend to speak for themselves. They embody a kind of "truth" which is, as Emerson put it, "its own testimony."

Before getting down to cases, however, we might usefully remind ourselves of a few of the things which poetic truth is *not*; and we might begin by noting that Carruth's target, advertising, as the main enemy of poetry ignores Clausen's alleged antithesis between "science" and "poetry"—an odd antithesis in any case, like saying "biophysics versus the humanities," "oil painting versus technology," or "the novel versus science." Why such a pointless antithesis? Perhaps because I. A. Richards once wrote controversially on this topic. My guess, however, is that it is because Clausen, like Matthew Arnold, mistakenly regards poetry as a vehicle of *religious* truth. That Clausen confuses poetry with religion seems plausible if we substitute in Clausen's hypothesis the term "religion" for "poetry": "the rise of science has had something to do with displacing religion as a publicly important vehicle for those truths that people accept as being centrally important." For poetry has never, as Clausen alleges it has, been "a publicly important vehicle for those truths we accept as centrally important." Indeed, for reasons which I will make clear a little later, religious truth and poetic truth, even though some poems may deal with religious themes, are quite distinct.

Nevertheless, let us take Clausen at his word, for a moment, and compare poetry with "science." Let us think of the meaning of a poem as being, like the formulation of a differential equation to describe the position of a moving particle or like the matching of a normal distribution curve to data, as a means of measurement. Let us go even a little further and, sticking with Clausen's vague term, "science," suppose that both "science" and "poetry" may be construed as methods of inquiry, each "field" with its specialized "body of knowledge." Although some of the resulting analogies we could draw between "science" and poetry are interesting, perhaps illuminating, the differences between "science" and poetry are far more significant than their similarities. They concern themselves with different kinds of truth.

The "truth" of a statement, as Clausen implicitly uses the term "truth" in connection with science, is ontological, having to do with what *is* and what is *not*. This type of truth is clearly defined by Philip Wheelwright in his study of poetic language, *The Burning Fountain*. There, in the chapter "Expressive Statement and Truth," Wheelwright describes it as follows: "Thus a statement is an assertorial type of meaning, and for practical purposes the sentences 'It is a statement' and 'It can be affirmed or denied' are interchangeable." The example of such a statement which Wheelwright uses is "The dog has broken loose." Wheelwright then goes on to contrast such "assertorial" statements with what he calls "poeto-statements," the type of nondeclarative utterance which we find frequently in poems, for example, "O Rose, thou art sick!" Such "poeto-statements" are characterized by what Wheelwright calls "assertorial lightness"; that is, they are not the kind of "utterance . . . to which one can respond with a *yes* or *no*." Wheelwright goes on to analyze various types of utterance which do not, like declarative propositions, demand the listener's "affirmation or denial," and he invites us to consider the following quotation from the Mundaka-Upanishad:

This is the truth. As from a blazing fire there fly forth thousands of sparks, like unto fire in substance, so are the various beings brought forth from the Imperishable and they return thither also.

Wheelwright asks:

In what sense and on what grounds, can the opening claim of truth be upheld? I am not asking whether or not the second sentence is actually true. What I am asking is: *If* that second sentence somehow expresses truth, as adherents of the Hindu philosophy believe it to do, in what sense does it do so?

Wheelwright then proceeds to answer his own question, invoking his own definition of "truth":

Since truth, as I have argued, is "that which ought, by one criterion or another, to be assented to," we can now see a little better the meaning of "poetic truth." A poetic utterance invites our imaginative assent, which is to say our depth assent, to some degree or other and in some context or other. So far as we yield such assent and gain insight in so doing, there is a real and valid sense in which we can speak of "poetic truth."

*　　*　　*　　*

Truth: "that which ought, by one criterion or another, to be assented to." In that one little word, "ought," Wheelwright implies just what Hayden Carruth does when Carruth complains about the lies of advertising. Wheelwright understands that "truth" can involve not just questions of yes or no, but questions of value. Poetic truth is truth about value, and it is this concern—with value rather than ontology or epistemology—which differentiates it from scientific truth. Frost put this difference as neatly as anybody when he used to remark to his students, "Science measures height, but can't measure worth. It never will." But "worth," value, in what sense? Monetary value? Ethical value? Moral value? Utilitarian value? To get at the question, let us look closely at a poem which is all about value, "Milk Weed," by Philip Levine:

> Remember how unimportant
> they seemed, growing loosely
> in the open fields we crossed
> on the way to school. We
> would carve wooden swords
> and slash at the luscious trunks
> until the white milk started
> and then flowed. Then we'd
> go on to the long day after
> day of the History of History
> or the tables of numbers and order
> as the clock slowly paid
> out the moments. The windows
> went dark first with rain
> and then snow, and then the days,
> then the years ran together and not
> one mattered more than
> another, and not one mattered.
>
> Two days ago I walked
> the empty woods, bent over,
> crunching through oak leaves,
> asking myself questions
> without answers. From somewhere
> a froth of seeds drifted by touched
> with gold in the last light
> of a lost day, going with
> the wind as they always did.

Rereading this poem, we immediately notice that its speaker/author is constantly making value judgments, that indeed the very structure of the poem is the dramatization of an action whereby he is sorting through experiences in order to discover and ultimately to clarify the relative values inherent there. The first stanza comprises a recollection of a childhood largely wasted indoors, in school, learning the attenuated "History of History"; the second stanza is set in the present, where we find the speaker outdoors, in direct, unmediated contact with "History," where, unlike the false environment of the schoolroom, "questions" are often "without answers." The glimpse of milkweed drifting in the late light staggers the poet with his realization of the magnitude of his loss; as a boy in the open field, slashing at the milkweed pods and stems, he had been at the very source of birth, generation, and perishing, at the source of creation itself, yet he had been too ignorant to recognize this.

The poem structures the relative values in the speaker's range of experience, and these values line up rather neatly. The structure is binary. Stanza one depicts past, childhood experience of low value: being indoors, being in school, being out of immediate contact with history, being given rote questions with rote answers, being ignorant. Stanza two, by contrast, depicts present, adult experience of higher value: being outdoors, being out of school and grown, being in immediate contact with history and natural process, asking oneself the right questions—questions without rote answers—knowing what *is* "important," even though such knowledge contains the consciousness of loss. Such an account does not, of course, do justice to the power and beauty of the poem. The image of the school windows going dark first with rain, then snow, is so terribly poignant, tells us so much about our lives. It reminds me that most of the time in grade school I was gazing out the window. What was happening outside, even the light on the clouds, seemed far more interesting than anything in the room. Perhaps the most vivid memories I have from grade school are of dire weather, of when the west would start hatching something so black that against it the trees outside seemed quarried out of chalk, of when the outdoors was plunged into night, of when the windows "went dark."

My accounting of the poem's assignment of value in terms of two lists, credit and debit, is, of course, deliberately overneat, but only in order to exhibit the existence of structure, to suggest how a good poem such as this one not only discovers the relative values in experience, but how it orders them into what we think of as a "style," measures them against one another in much the same way that a good painting by, say, Edward Hopper, makes us notice qualities of light by means of their relationship to one another within the composition.

"Style." It is one of those words which, when used conventionally, has a meaning we take virtually for granted, but which, when isolated from a context, becomes suddenly slippery. To understand the sense in which I intend my usage of this word, consider how, if "personality" is a form of style, an individual's personality or "style" reveals itself in terms of action, as a series of choices which are, we know, the result of what that person values: in dress, speech, politics, friends, play, and so on. In art, in literature, indeed, in all human action, style is the calculus of value.

A poem, if it has any coherence whatsoever, attributes a style to the experience which it depicts, by composing the complex values of that experience in a structure whereby those values illuminate one another: what is "important" is brought into relief; what is less important receives less notice. Value, in art, is generally expressed in terms of emphasis, as indeed Levine's opening line reminds us, in the word "unimportant." The mere act of weighing "importance," of bringing something to attention—a milkweed plant, a window gone dark—is an act of valuation. What kind of valuation? If the Levine poem is any indication, it is not exactly moral or ethical valuation, nor is it economic or utilitarian. It is more subtle. It has to do with the value of things in themselves. It has to do with the act of significantly noticing one's experience—*significantly* because this action involves *choosing* what to notice or to ignore—this act or series of them carried over into language. Indeed, as William Stafford's well-documented approach to writing would argue, the acts of noticing which attend poetic composition are, in part, achieved *by means of* language.

Wallace Stevens, likewise, represents the exercise of language itself as a form of action in which what we see and what we say are mutually dependent:

> I placed a jar in Tennessee,
> And round it was, upon a hill.
> It made the slovenly wilderness
> Surround that hill.

Here, the jar is representative of any set of terms—such as lines, points, or words—invented by the human imagination and superimposed as a sort of coordinate system upon the world. It is through the very action of "placing" such "jars" that we not only order the world mathematically—map it— but also valuate our experience. As an example of this, consider Stevens's beautiful lines from "The Idea of Order at Key West": "It was her voice that made / The sky acutest at its vanishing." Obviously these lines have something to do with the way in which, on a clear day, the blue sky pales and sharpens the closer our gaze draws toward the horizon, at which point our gaze craves to go over the horizon. Equally obvious, such aspects of our experience tend to go insufficiently noticed. But once noticed, the "acuteness" of the sky "at its vanishing" adds to our total fund of experience. Indeed, such an act of precise, fresh noticing is an act of valuation: it implies that even the subtlest, most seemingly peripheral aspects of our experience may be worth our attention.

*   *   *   *

From this example and from the Levine poem it should be apparent why good poetry depends on much more than mere technique and how the term "technique" when applied to poetry can be actually misleading. Poetry depends also upon the capacity of its author to pay good attention to the world, to learn from it, to take an interest in it, to be at times surprised by it, and to observe it accurately. A good poem is a test of the capacity of its author. Just as, in the plot of a realistic story, novel, or movie, the choices which the protagonist makes eventually give us a clear sense of that person's character—his capacity for malice, courage, generosity, and so on— so does a poem, through the action of its author matching choices of language to choices of value, choices between what or what not to notice and bring to attention, give us a clear indication of its author's ethos and total alertness. It would be simplistic, of course, and would fly in the face of vast amounts of biographical evidence, to suggest that to be a good poet one must be a good person. But if we look at the Levine poem we must think that the ethos of the author has at least something to do with the poem's quality. The poem is not whining, not bitter, not pedantic, not sneering, but is informed by a wise, rather rueful perspective. And we would have to agree,

I think, that the aspects of experience which it enables us to more fully notice and to judge are those aspects which an intelligent, curious, critical, compassionate, sensitive, educated, alert person would deem worthy of attention. To put the matter in Wheelwright's terms: "Milk Weed" is an excellent poem not only because it structures the values of our experience into a style, but because this "style" is one to which we feel we *ought* to "give assent." In other words, "style," per se, is no guarantee of any worth.

All art, including bad art, from Disneyland to Barbie Dolls to TV beer commercials glamorizing blue-collar life, asserts one style or another and would attribute that style to our experience. But as the paraphernalia of the Barbie Doll world would testify, some styles are bad. Indeed, as Carruth would probably argue, most of the ways in which the commercial world would style our lives are bad. Why? For precisely the reason which Carruth gives. They lie about value.

Truth above value: it is hardly surprising that this subject has become an almost obsessive one in modern and postmodern poetry. In a world where everything is for sale— where "to sell yourself" is now an expression we toss down without even blinking—in an environment in which every aspect of our experience, from making love to brushing our teeth to staying physically fit, has been appropriated by commerce and transformed into a marketable product, the *actual* value, the "true value" (how conscious I am that "true value" is already the trademarked name of a franchise) of every part of our lives becomes both harder to discern and to express. As is well known, it is just this corruption of value by commerce which became, in the second half of Pound's life, an obsession. And we are all too familiar with Pound's story.

Pound longed for an ideal culture—he claimed to have found evidences of such cultures in the past—in which the economic or "market value" of artifacts accurately reflected their true value. As we know, it was his belief that the lending of money—usury—was and is the prime cause for the grotesque discrepancy we often find between market value and actual value, a discrepancy which, Pound claimed, like Carruth, has all but ruined us. We remember Pound's famous line in the forty-fifth of his *Cantos*, "with usura the line grows thick"—Pound's notion that one could calculate the interest rate in an economy by how thick the artist's line. The higher the interest rate, the thicker—that is, the more careless—it would be. In other words, the higher the interest rate, the more we are apt to find people doing schlock work. And, indeed, as Hugh Kenner has pointed out, if we look at tract housing and consider the relation between that housing and the banking industry, there is a disturbingly prophetic quality to Pound's dictum.

As both the Levine poem and Stevens's "Anecdote of the Jar" would suggest, however, it is possible to elucidate structures of value without linking them with economics. In fact, I think it is preferable to consider questions of aesthetic or ethical value outside the context of economics, and that it was in his attempt to link such questions to economics that Pound went not just badly wrong; he went virtually insane. For one thing, to make such a linkage is to fall prey to the ever-tempting fallacy of trying to quantify quality, in this case, by putting a dollar value on it. A more serious limitation in Pound's approach to questions of value, however, and a clue as to why so much of Pound's own later poetry is failed poetry, is Pound's constant appeal, both implicit and explicit, to some external authority or other to ratify a system of value— the authority of culture. Pound is continually, by adducing examples of beautiful work from allegedly healthier past cultures, regarding the relative values of things as if those values could only be received, instead of regarding value as something which can be made or discovered.

I am, of course, aware that when I said earlier that a good poem "enables us to notice and to judge . . . those aspects of experience which an intelligent, curious, compassionate, sensitive, alert person would deem worthy of attention," I am treating the knowledge of "what is worthy" as received knowledge. Poetically, however, such knowledge has little force— does not, to use Wheelwright's language, compel our "depth assent"—when it is complacently presented as dogma, as a static truth. In order to compel our assent, truth in a poem must be, as that tired saying has it, "earned." It must be discovered afresh through the very process of composition— through action by which some structure, some set of connections, is revealed. And it is our sense of such action, of the poet working alone in his or her poem, which will lend that poem the authenticity which makes us assent to its poetic "truth," to that clarification of value which an achieved poem ultimately delivers.

As an example of what I mean by "authenticity" and why such authenticity is a precondition of "poetic truth," consider the following poem by Nancy Willard:

Walking Poem

How beautifully the child I carry on my back
teaches me to become a horse.
How quickly I learn to stay
between shafts, blinders, and whips,
bearing the plough

and the wagon loaded with hay,
or to break out of trot and run
till we're flying through cold streams.
He who kicks my commands
knows I am ten times his size

and that I am servant to small hands.
It is in mowed fields I move best,
watching the barn grow toward me,
the child quiet, his sleep piled like hay
on my back as we slip over the dark hill

and I carry the sun away.

Instead of thinking of this piece as a well manufactured, seamless picture with a premeditated meaning, let us instead regard it as a form of action dramatizing a process of discovery. Of course, unless we ask the author, we have no way to reconstruct the actual order of events in this poem's composition. But we feel a sense of the composition process—of action leading to dawning discovery—as we read and reread. As is nearly always the case in the achieved short lyric, the seeds of the poem's final discovery, after it makes what in workshop parlance is often called its "turn," are concealed in the beginning of the poem: it has something to do with the reciprocal bond between mother and child, and with power. Who is in charge of whom? Who is obeying whom? Willard reenacts her ride, in lazy, cantering rhythms, plunging herself so wholly into the part of "a horse" ("It is in mowed fields I move best") that she was in perfect harmony with her son's playacting. The poem rides over "cold streams" and "mowed fields" until, in its last lines, it majestically deepens and makes its discovery: the speaker becomes both her child and her adult self, simultaneously. So intense, at this point in the poem, is her remembered empathy with her sleepy child in the pack, that she can imagine how the barn must look to *him*—not as if they were moving toward it but as if *it* were magically "growing toward" *them*. Similarly, as they descend the shady side of the hill, and the lowering sun is abruptly cut off by the hill's crest, the last glimpse which she imagines the child might have of the sun makes it appear as if the sun were being towed down the sky toward the horizon and "carried" below it, just as the sun daily appears to us as if *it* were moving, circling the earth. The revelation of this double vision is timed within the poem to coincide exactly with a remembered reversal of the balance of power in the game between mother and child, embodied in the last line in the pun on "son"; the child, just before he nods off, sees the *sun* being carried away, when, in fact, *he* (the son) is being carried away. The suggestiveness of this reversal is vast: that she is to him as is the earth itself, which, by its turning, brings on day and night. She, in her benign but absolute power over the child, recapitulates the earth's diurnal rhythms, a power which connects her with the earth itself, with the universe.

What are the values which this poem explores, and how are these values structured? "Walking Poem" contrasts the value of child's play and pretend power, on the one hand, against the value of adult playfulness and of real power and responsibility on the other. The poem celebrates both; but it values the adult perspective more highly than the childhood perspective. It does not, however, deny the childhood perspective. It merely circumscribes it, is an enlargement of it. Adults can play *and* be responsible. Indeed, the poem suggests that gracefully dispatched responsibility may be the ultimate adult form of play. The way in which "Walking Poem" structures these values is not quite as cut and dried as is the two-part, antithetical structure of Levine's "Milk Weed." Willard's structure is narrative. With the poem's very opening words, "How beautifully," the poem announces the value of child's play. It then proceeds, more or less continuously, to deepen and intensify that value. It is just when the child falls asleep that the poem leaps into the adult perspective, placing all the preceding description in the richer context of adult knowledge, adult love.

As this explication suggests, the poem's main discovery is a set of metaphoric connections, connections which, spelled out explicitly, lose the mysterious, vast sense of revelation and joy which makes the poem's ending so powerful. But it is also the *action* which led to this discovery—action which took place during the poem's composition and which is reflected in the dramatic timing of that discovery in the poem's final version—which lends this set of discovered connections even greater force, compelling our assent. Such dramatization seems—Frost would argue that it *is* and has to be in a good poem—completely authentic; and it is in such authenticity that the "poetic truth" of a poem like Willard's differs from religious truth. Willard's poem does not deliver us some complacently predigested, didactic valuation of human existence. It does not, for example, announce to us, with armchair assurance, what we already believe—that "motherhood is good," that "empathy with your children is good," or that "play is good," though of course such notions are part of the poem's overall import. Instead, the poem dramatizes the authentic discovery of the relative values in such experience.

We find this same type of drama—the drama of valuation through noticing—in every achieved poem, for example in Reg Saner's remarkable poem "The Day the Air Was on Fire," a poem all about noticing and one in which "noticing" is presented explicitly as a form of action, as an intense and almost devotional kind of work whereby bits of value, of beauty, are gleaned, like Williams's "saxifrage," literally out of rock:

> All afternoon neither of us said
> "This air's on fire," though both felt it
> and felt in sunlight like that, death
> was impossible, or if possible, overrated,
> even trivial. The sky kept showing off
> in all colors, each of them blue
> and we trekked that enormous plateau
> whose tundra darkened or flared in one broad
> autumnal crackle of burnt orange, then gold,
> drifting under islands of cumulus
> as if somebody'd laid out the pelt
> from a sunset. Toward the nearest of two

schist cairns studding the highest stretches
we knelt and touched late gentian corollas,
still half bud. "How long till first snow?"
Days, not weeks. But with outcrops insisting
the last word should be rocks, then flaking
and falling away from that, we noticed
how each tuft put them to use
improvising soil from palmfuls of grit,
saying "If not this season, the next—
perhaps the one after," and coming on
very small, coming on uphill,
against everything.

Saner's poem represents poem-making—poetry—as a form of action, and as the poem proceeds it conveys to us an almost physical sense of exertion—in its springy rhythm, in its resolute forward movement, in the textures and tactility of its words as they are stressed, bent, wielded, and in the predicates, "studding . . . knelt . . . touched . . . insisting . . . flaking and falling . . . improvising . . . coming on . . . coming on," which lend us our sense of the entire poem as one extended verb. Indeed, the complex connections which this poem traces are implicated in this very action: the acts of noticing by which Saner builds his poem parallel precisely the tundra's bent to improvise soil so that it can support, in the face of all the odds, gentians. In this harsh environment, the gentians would seem to be so unlikely as to be wholly unnecessary. Why try to grow them *here*, of all places? Saner leaves the answer implicit; but it is clear, and it amounts to a rhetorical question: why try to grow *anything anywhere*? The gentians are no more or less gratuitous than his own poem must be. Our bent to improvise beauty through attention to the world and to language is the human equivalent to the insistence of the gentians that they simply exist: it is the insistence, "against everything," on the value of Being, on Being for its own sake. Interest in the world, Saner's poem dramatizes, is the most fundamental form of love toward it. And by "interest" I do not mean the compulsive "interest" we might take in a headache or in lower back pains. I mean *voluntary* interest. Indeed, even children know intuitively that attention given voluntarily *is* love. It affirms and esteems their existence. Likewise, Saner's action in making his poem, and nature's repeated effort to produce gentians under nearly im-

possible conditions, are, through their "voluntary" quality—
that is, their very (seeming) superfluity—a form of absolute
love, a praise of creation for its own sake, perhaps the only
authentic form of worship.

*   *   *   *

"The Day the Air Was on Fire," although it touches on certain grand religious themes, demonstrates in its capacity for
dramatization how poetic discourse differs, in *its* method of
discriminating value, from religious doctrine. Whereas religious doctrine delivers us an already discovered, accepted,
codified system of values—official truth—poems like those of
Saner, Willard, and Levine carry with them a kind of authenticity which the truth of religious doctrine tries to assert but
can never quite achieve. Every organized religion is, of course,
perpetually anxious about this. We need only reread Jonathan
Edwards's sermon "Sinners in the Hands of an Angry God"
or watch any vigorous televised church sermon for evidence
of how terribly aware religious institutions are that, given
the revealed, settled, certified nature of religious truth, it
must be constantly revitalized, dramatized, made to seem
fresh. This is why, over and over again, religions resort to the
authenticity of art, whether by Tintoretto or Bach, to refur-
bish their truth. Without the rhetoric of art, such "truth"
would far less efficiently compel, to borrow Wheelwright's
term, our "assent."

"Authenticity." Just how thoroughly commercialized mass
culture has corrupted our language may be indicated by the
degree to which even this word has been debased. Despite its
existential elaboration culminating in Lionel Trilling's elegant
analysis, "authenticity" has, thanks largely to the psychology,
self-help, group-therapy industry, come to be associated too
often with merely an aggressive, shameless sincerity. When
we use the word "authenticity" we find ourselves in a position much like that of Pound in *Mauberley*, where he laments,
"We see το καλὸν [The Beautiful] / Decreed in the market
place." We understand that Carruth's accusation that "lying
has become a way of life, very nearly now *the* way of life," is,
like Pound's lament, about much more than the mere market
value of things. Carruth is referring to lies about value in

every domain of our lives—lies about how we should direct our attention, how we should work, how we should raise our children, how we should love, how we should spend our time. We can begin to understand why a truly achieved poem like Saner's has such abiding value, why the art of poetry will persist so long as there is one person left who is not satisfied with experience as it is styled for us by committee, by network, or by market research.

"Authenticity." The word comes from the Greek *authentes*, which means "one who does anything with his own hand." Our sense of the value of a well-made poem, like our delight in any expertly handmade artifact—a piece of stoneware, a piece of jewelry—is intimately connected with our sense that it is not mass produced, not stamped out by machine, that the decisions which went into its shaping were not those of a committee, a corporation, or a survey, but were the decisions of a single, passionate individual—the author—acting alone within the conventions of the art, and that this author used the best materials available, exerted care and judgment at every turn, and exerted as much time and effort as was necessary to make the artifact as well as it could be made. The best materials: as I have already suggested, the material of which a poem is made is not just language: it is human experience noticed in language. Of course, the fact that a given poem has been based upon an actual experience, like some certificate proving that an artifact is handmade, is no guarantee of its quality. In order that it have beauty, it must, in its textures, bear the mysterious but unmistakable mark of individual craftsmanship, the residue of human touch. We must sense the action which went into its making; because a good poem is as much a form of action—a serious, responsible action carried out within the limits of convention—as is the conducting of a friendship or a marriage. Authoritative style, good style, confronts us not just with truth about value: that truth has been authenticated. When we read Saner's poem, instead of being told how the values in our experience should be structured—that the momentary, random beauty of sunsets (what Saner elsewhere has labeled "pure calendar art"), compared to the subtler, more difficult and deeply imagined beauty-in-hardship epitomized by the gentians flowering in rock, is rather specious and rather trite—we actually watch the poet, in his poem, in the very act of choosing and weighing, looking here and there, chipping at the world with his words to test its substance, its values, until the poem is left. We watch him at work alone, making.

Although all art is strictly bound by convention, in this era of mass culture it remains one of the very few precincts left where significant individual freedom of action—true authenticity—is possible, where an individual can create some valid style. Poetic truth is a truth of style, and this is why, today, we return so longingly, with such gratitude, to a good poem, like Saner's, as we do to any artifact that is finely made, that is truly authored: to handle it, heft it, sniff it, pat it, repeat it, recite it, to keep it in view, to wear it and to memorize it, enlarging our capacity to value life itself.

Index

Altieri, Charles, 45, 144
Ammons, A. R., 11
Arnold, Matthew, 171
Ashbery, John, 4–5, 9, 32, 40, 59,
  61, 62, 64–65, 67–70, 116–17
Auden, W. H., 12, 63, 76–78, 84,
  144

Baraka, Imamu, 9, 11
Beardsley, M. C., 98
Bell, Marvin, 28, 101
Beowulf poet, 140
Bergson, Henri, 165
Berryman, John, 26
Blake, William, 142, 172
Bloom, Harold, 9–11, 15–16, 18
Bly, Robert, 9, 28–29, 31, 54–55,
  60, 66–67
Booth, Wayne, 100
Brautigan, Richard, 166–69
Breslin, Paul, 10, 30, 58–59, 66–
  67, 69

Carlyle, Thomas, 68
Carney, Raymond, 99–100, 103
Carruth, Hayden, 170–72, 177,
  183–84
Cervantes, Miguel de, 118
Clausen, Christopher, 170–71
Coleridge, Samuel Taylor, 2, 38,
  110, 126, 134, 140
Creeley, Robert, 48, 140

Dickey, James, 9
Dickinson, Emily, 147–48, 150,
  152, 156–58, 160
Donne, John, 140

Edwards, Jonathan, 183
Eliot, T. S., 3, 11–12, 15, 32, 63,
  115, 136
Emerson, Ralph Waldo, 10, 15–16
Enzensburger, Hans Magnus,
  82–83

Forché, Carolyn, 10, 16, 27, 75–
  76, 79–80, 82, 84–88, 90–91
Freud, Sigmund, 159, 162–66
Frost, Robert, 2, 5, 13, 38, 44, 70–
  71, 98–99, 101–3, 105, 107, 109,
  114, 116, 128, 170, 173
Frumkin, Gene, 60–62
Frye, Northrop, 63–64, 96, 97

Gage, John, 46
Gildner, Gary, 17–18, 23–24, 27,
  105–9
Ginsberg, Allen, 9, 16, 80–85
Glück, Louise, 11, 16
Graham, Jorie, 28, 40–44, 64–67

Hall, Donald, 69
Hardy, Thomas, 5
Hartman, Charles O., 45, 87,
  92–109
Hass, Robert, 45, 67–70, 157
Hawthorne, Nathaniel, 2
Hillyer, Robert, 11–16, 18
Hopkins, Gerard Manley, 144, 152
Hopper, Edward, 148, 175
Hughes, Ted, 49
Hugo, Richard, 5, 7, 16, 24, 26, 34,
  119, 122–24, 153–58, 160
Hulme, T. E., 28, 45–46, 145

Jung, C. G., 29–30

Keats, John, 26–27, 49–51, 54–55,
  98, 112
Kenner, Hugh, 178
Kilmer, Joyce, 95–96, 115–17
Kinnell, Galway, 9, 16, 28, 30–31,
  51–56
Kipling, Rudyard, 83
Kooser, Ted, 23–24, 26
Kunitz, Stanley, 54

Lacan, Jacques, 157, 159–60
Legman, G., 162–63

Levertov, Denise, 16, 18–23, 26
Levine, Philip, 173–78, 183
Lifshin, Lyn, 168–69
Logan, John, 119–22
Lowell, Robert, 26, 54
Ludvigson, Susan, 35–39, 43

MacLeish, Archibald, 47
Mallarmé, Stéphane, 136, 140, 144
Matthews, William, 28, 71–72
Mazzaro, Jerome, 9, 10
Mendelson, Edward, 14
Merwin, W. S., 28–31
Monet, Claude, 148

Neruda, Pablo, 60–62, 83

Pack, Robert, 31
Pinsky, Robert, 18, 45–59, 67
Plumly, Stanley, 23, 27, 35, 37, 45, 48, 103–5, 107–8
Poe, Edgar Allan, 143
Pope, Alexander, 24, 140, 143–44
Poulin, A., 9, 26, 119
Pound, Ezra, 11–12, 25–26, 32, 45–46, 63, 115, 177–78, 183

Rich, Adrienne, 9, 78–79, 84, 86
Robinson, Edwin Arlington, 13
Roethke, Theodore, 54, 166–67

Sandburg, Carl, 109
Saner, Reg, 181–85
Sexton, Anne, 117

Simic, Charles, 89–90
Simpson, Louis, 31, 56–57, 84–88, 160
Smith, Barbara Herrnstein, 80, 94–98, 113–14, 117, 119, 123, 143
Snyder, Gary, 9, 34
Stafford, William, 5, 16, 28, 39–40, 43, 73, 87, 118, 150–52, 175
Stevens, Wallace, 5, 35, 44, 81–83, 92–94, 96–98, 100–101, 104–5, 108–9, 111–13, 115–16, 121, 126, 133–39, 143, 175–76, 178

Trilling, Lionel, 14–15, 183

Valéry, Paul, 5, 131, 133, 143, 166, 168

Walker, David, 70
Wheelwright, Philip, 62, 170–72, 177, 183
Whitman, Walt, 5, 94, 119, 124
Wilbur, Richard, 9, 31, 35
Willard, Nancy, 179–81
Williams, William Carlos, 25, 116
Wimsatt, W. K., 98
Wittgenstein, Ludwig, 3
Wordsworth, William, 5, 14, 24, 34–35, 38, 77, 99, 109–10, 124, 148, 151, 156–60
Wright, James, 9–10, 25

Yeats, William Butler, 13, 113

Permissions